Competition Law in Australia

Competition Law in Australia

Third Edition

Lynden Griggs
Jane Nielsen

This book was originally published as a monograph in the International Encyclopaedia of Laws/Competition Law.

Founding Editor: Roger Blanpain
General Editor: Frank Hendrickx
Volume Editors: Francesco Denozza & Alberto Toffoletto

Wolters Kluwer

Published by:
Kluwer Law International B.V.
PO Box 316
2400 AH Alphen aan den Rijn
The Netherlands
E-mail: international-sales@wolterskluwer.com
Website: lrus.wolterskluwer.com

Sold and distributed in North, Central and South America by:
Wolters Kluwer Legal & Regulatory U.S.
7201 McKinney Circle
Frederick, MD 21704
United States of America
Email: customer.service@wolterskluwer.com

Sold and distributed in all other countries by:
Air Business Subscriptions
Rockwood House
Haywards Heath
West Sussex
RH16 3DH
United Kingdom
Email: international-customerservice@wolterskluwer.com

ISBN 978-94-035-2272-2

e-Book: ISBN 978-94-035-2273-9
web-PDF: ISBN 978-94-035-2274-6

The Authors

Dr Lynden Griggs has a PhD in Published Work from Bond University in Australia. This body of work critically examines the doctrinal coherence of the Torrens System of Land Registration. He is a Fellow of the Higher Education Research Development Society of Australasia. His principal areas of interest are land law, competition law, and consumer law. He has numerous publications in these areas, including co-authoring *Australian Real Property Law* and *Cases and Materials on Australian Property Law*. Griggs wrote all parts except for *Dominant Undertakings' Prohibited Practices* in Part II.

Dr Jane Nielsen is an Associate Professor in Law at the University of Tasmania in Australia. She has an Honours degree in Law and a PhD from the University of Tasmania in Australia. She is admitted as a barrister and solicitor of the Supreme Court of Tasmania, High Court of Australia and the Federal Courts of Australia. Her principal areas of interest are competition law, intellectual property law and tort law. She has also written extensively on issues associated with genetic diagnostic testing, the ethical, legal and social issues associated with genomics research and regulation and the regulation of innovative health technologies. Nielsen wrote *Dominant Undertakings' Prohibited Practices* in Part II.

The Authors

Table of Contents

List of Abbreviations

ABLR	Australian Business Law Review
ACCC	Australian Competition and Consumer Commission
ACT	Australian Competition Tribunal
AJCCL	Australian Journal of Competition and Consumer Law
All ER	All England Law Reports
ALR	Australian Law Reports
ASIC	Australian Securities and Investments Commission
ATPR	Australian Trade Practices Reports
ATPR (Com)	Australian Trade Practices Reports (Commission)
ATPR (Digest)	Australian Trade Practices Reports (Digest)
CCA	Competition and Consumer Act 2010
CCLJ	Competition and Consumer Law Journal
CLR	Commonwealth Law Reports
FCA	Federal Court of Australia
FCR	Federal Court Reports
FLR	Federal Law Reports
KB	Kings Bench
QB	Queens Bench
SASR	South Australian State Reports
CCA	Competition and Consumer Act 2010
TPA	Trade Practices Act 1974
TPC	Trade Practices Commission
TPR	Trade Practices Reports
TPLJ	Trade Practices Law Journal
WLR	Weekly Law Reports

List of Abbreviations

General Introduction

§1. General Background of the Country

1. Australia is an island continent located in the southern hemisphere. It is situated between the Pacific and Indian oceans. Much of the population of Australia (approximately 25 million) is located on the coastal areas with the major population centres (Sydney, Melbourne and Brisbane) situated on the Eastern seaboard. The inland of Australia is generally dry and arid. The majority of Australians are of an Anglo-Saxon origin with the dominant culture, language and customs similar to those of other Anglo-Saxon countries such as the United States, Canada and England. Today, however, recent migrants are just as likely to be from Asian regions.

The political system of Australia is based on democratically elected governments. Australia today is a Federation comprising of a national government, six state governments and two internal territories. Australia is also a constitutional monarchy with allegiance to the Queen of Great Britain. The national government is formed by the party with the majority of seats in the lower house of Parliament. The leader of that party serves as Prime Minister assisted by a Cabinet consisting of members from both the lower house of Parliament (called the House of Representatives) and the upper house of Parliament (called the Senate). At the Commonwealth level, general elections must be held at least once every three years. In 1901, the adoption of the Australian constitution led to the formation of Federation and the creation of Australia with its constituent states and territories. At the time of Federation, options would have included having a unitary form of government, with the central government responsible for the entire nation. This would have seen the colonies that existed prior to the Federation ceasing. Thus, to obtain the support of the colonies or the states as they became known, a Federal form of government was adopted. This sees a national government with the power to create laws for the entire country in respect of certain designated matters, such as trading corporations. Outside of the designated powers within the Australian constitution, the states retained residual powers to legislate. Increasingly, the Commonwealth is seen as having more centralized power, particularly through funding arrangements than the states. All states and territories are democratically elected.

§2. The Economic System

2. Australia is a mixed free-market economy. Increasingly industries that in the past would have been conducted by the government have been privatized (such as telecommunications and electricity delivery). However, the State still plays a significant role in certain areas, for example, postal delivery, though this is increasingly under examination. The major industries of Australia are tourism, education, financial services and mining. Australia is also a major exporter of beef, wool, sugar, wheat and a number of vegetables. The major mining exports include iron ore, gold, lead, copper, silver, aluminium and bauxite.

§3. The Legal System

3. The legal system in Australia is reflective of its culture. This culture, based on a largely free-market ethos, recognizes the protection of the person and property as paramount. As a country, the rule of law is observed with this meaning that all people irrespective of race, religion or financial resource are equal before the law. There are a number of institutional players within the legal system in Australia. The Commonwealth Parliament has the power to make laws as prescribed by the constitution of Australia, and if state or territory governments make laws inconsistent with the Commonwealth, the Commonwealth laws will prevail. The senior legal officer of the country is the Attorney-General. The Commonwealth, through the constitution, has established a series of Federal Courts as well as the High Court of Australia. The High Court of Australia is the highest-ranking court in the country. Each state also establishes its own hierarchy of courts. Generally, this will include a Magistrates Court, a District Court and finally a Supreme Court of the state. Smaller jurisdictions will omit the District Court. Also critical to the legal system in Australia is the legal profession. In Australia, this is undertaken by people with formal university qualifications with prescriptive canons relating to conduct and ethics. Australia is an adversarial system whereby both parties in dispute are represented by members of the legal profession before the relevant courts. There is also a very comprehensive system whereby people can challenge the decision of administrative regulators to administrative tribunals. For example, at the Commonwealth level, the Administrative Appeals Tribunal has been established. This allows for the review of decisions made by Commonwealth government departments.

§4. Historical Background of Antitrust Law

4. In Australia, competition law (as it is known in this jurisdiction) is of a relatively recent origin. The first Act specifically regulating competition law matters was not passed until 1965 (*Trade Practices Act 1965*), though in 1906, the then newly established Federal Parliament did pass the *Australian Industries Preservation Act*. This sought to prohibit restraints of trade or commerce that was to the detriment of the public. However, it was largely unsuccessful in achieving those objectives. Because of this, anticompetitive practices (such as collusive behaviour) were rampant within Australian industry. With the limited utility of the legislation, Australian authorities were reliant on common law doctrines, such as restraint of trade to reign in behaviour that was seen to be adverse to the economy. This 1965 legislation was invalidated on constitutional grounds[1] and replaced by the *Restrictive Trade Practices Act 1971*. The origins of the present legislation stem from the enactment in 1974 of the *Trade Practices Act 1974* (TPA) with this replaced by the *Competition and Consumer Act 2010* (CCA). The Act is a mixture of legal and economic concepts and definitions. The objects of the Act are to promote effective competition and encourage fair trading and the protection of consumers.[2]

1. *Strickland v. Rocla Concrete Pipes* (1971) 124 CLR 468.
2. See s 2 *Competition and Consumer Act 2010*.

Part I. The Structure of Antitrust Law and Its Enforcement

Chapter 1. Sources of Antitrust Law

§1. National Sources

5. The primary source of competition law in Australia is the *Competition and Consumer Act 2010* (CCA). This is Commonwealth legislation. However, in the mid-1990s, states and territories all enacted mirror legislation to what is now the CCA,[3] which allows the extension of the competition law principles to non-corporate entities, something which would not have been possible without the mirror legislation. The regulatory body charged with administering the CCA is the Australian Competition and Consumer Commission (ACCC).

6. The functions of the ACCC are detailed in Part II of the Act. These functions include prosecuting breaches of anticompetitive conduct as well as arbitrating disputes between a firm seeking access to an essential service and the provider of that service (*see* Parts IIIA and Part XIC of the CCA), legal research, law reform and critically in terms of competition law, assessing applications for authorizations and notification of anticompetitive conduct.

7. As noted in paragraph 6, the ACCC has the power to arbitrate a dispute between an essential service and a person seeking access to that service. For example, the process involves a person seeking access to a service applying to the National Competition Council (NCC). The NCC is established under Part IIIA of the Act with its mandate directed towards policy formation and consideration of access disputes. If the NCC recommends that access be provided, the facility owner and the third party can then seek to have the ACCC arbitrate any dispute about the price or means of access. Parties are able to appeal from this to the Australian Competition Tribunal (ACT). The ACT is empowered under Part III of the legislation to hear appeals from decisions of the regulator. The role of the ACCC and the ACT in resolving access disputes and hearing and determining applications for authorization and notification sees these two institutions as a source of competition law.

3. See Part XIA *Competition and Consumer Act 2010.*

§2. International Sources

8. International sources inform the debate surrounding competition law in Australia. Decisions emanating from the European Union and the American courts can be cited in Australian judgments and the policy deliberations and directions given from overseas will contribute to the richness of competition law in Australia. The ACCC will also work with international regulators where the anticompetitive conduct has a global or multi-national dimension. The ACCC is also a member of the International Competition Network (ICN). Australia and the US have also formally recognized through a treaty that they will exchange evidence on a reciprocal basis (Australia–US Treaty – antitrust enforcement assistance, 1999). The ACCC has signed agreements with the following countries (*see* https://www.accc.gov.au/about-us/international-relations/treaties-agreements for the current list):

- Canada
- Chinese Taipei
- Fiji Islands
- India
- Republic of Korea
- New Zealand
- Papua New Guinea
- United Kingdom
- Japan
- Philipines
- European Commission
- United States of America.

§3. Secondary Sources

I. Regulations

9. A number of secondary sources assist in the interpretation and understanding of competition law. Regulations enacted pursuant to the CCA (*Competition and Consumer Act Regulations 2010*) work to assist practitioners in the process of the administration of competition law. Industry Codes can also be prescribed under section 51AD of the Act. There are currently five prescribed mandatory industry codes (noted below), and there is also a voluntary Food and Grocery Code of Conduct:

- Franchising Code
- Oil Code
- Horticulture Code
- Unit Pricing Code
- Wheat Port Code.

II. Guidelines

10. The ACCC issues many guidelines to assist business in understanding their obligations and the process that the ACCC takes in reviewing mergers, investigating cartels and seeking formal clearance. The guidelines include:

- Merger Review Guidelines 2008
- Media Merger Guidelines 2017
- Informal Review Merger Process Guidelines 2013
- Authorisation Guidelines 2017
- Guidelines on Concerted Practices
- ACCC immunity and cooperation policy for cartel conduct
- Small Business Collective Bargaining Guidelines
- Guidelines on Misuse of Market Power.

§4. Sources Relation and Hierarchy

11. As noted, the primary source is the legislation established by the Federal Parliament (CCA). The regulations assist the process, and the guidelines inform the participants. Delegated legislation is known as subordinate legislation. In this sense, the subordinate legislation must be consistent with the CCA, and any inconsistency can be challenged through the Federal court system.

§5. Role and Authority of Precedents

12. Precedent plays a critical role in the Australian legal system. The *ratio decidendi* of one case can be used to resolve a later case, where that later case involves similar facts. The hierarchy of courts is also important. The High Court of Australia binds all courts, with the Full Federal Court binding single judges of the Federal Court. A lower court is bound to follow the authority of a higher court, even though it may disapprove of the decision.

Chapter 2. Scope of Application

§1. Territorial Reach

13. Territorial reach must be considered in light of the Federal system of government operating in Australia. The Australian constitution provides for limited power to the Federal Parliament. For competition law, this power critically extends to foreign corporations, trading corporations, financial corporations, corporations incorporated in a territory and holding companies of the above corporations.[4]

14. Due to the states and territories having applied the competition law principles to their own jurisdictions, the reach of competition law now extends to non-corporate entities such as sole traders, partnerships and unincorporated associations. Each state and territory has vested all matters that arise under the Code to the resolution of the Federal Courts and the regulatory reach of the ACCC. The CCA can apply to the Commonwealth and State Crowns (sections 2A/2B).

15. Other constitutional bases for applying competition law principles to a transaction include where:

- the conduct is between Australia and an overseas jurisdiction;
- between the states;
- between the states and the territories or between the territories; and
- where there is a supply of goods or services to the Commonwealth.[5]

16. The principles outlined in paragraph 15 are of less importance today, given the application of competition law principles to natural persons (*see* paragraph 14).

17. Once the application of the competition law principles are found to apply, the next question is whether the reach of the legislation is to conduct just occurring in Australia or does it extend beyond this. This question is answered by the definition of the market in section 4E of the CCA. Currently, this indicates that Part IV of the CCA (the competition law rules) is only concerned with markets in Australia.

18. Presently, if the conduct does occur overseas but affects competition in Australia, section 5(1) of the CCA indicates that the Australian authorities and institutions will have jurisdiction to consider the matter, provided the requirements of this provision are met. The notion of extraterritoriality is quite limited in Australia. We do not have anything equivalent to the effects doctrine that applies in the European community or the United States of America. The issue has rarely arisen for litigation in Australia. Currently, section 5(1) of the *Competition and Consumer Act* provides that:

4. Definition of a corporation – s, 4(1) *Competition and Consumer Act 2010.*
5. Section 6 *Competition and Consumer Act 2010.*

> Part IV ... extend[s] to the engaging in conduct outside Australia by:
>
> a. bodies corporate incorporated or carrying on business within Australia; or
> b. Australian citizens; or
> c. persons ordinarily resident within Australia.

§2. Special Sectors

19. There is a special regime for telecommunications contained with the CCA. The Federal Parliament considered that the complexity of this industry and the degree of horizontal and vertical integration necessitated a specific regime for this industry. Accordingly, Part XIB of the CCA applies to anticompetitive conduct that involves both a 'carrier' and 'carriage service provider' and with such conduct occurring in a telecommunications market. Section 151AK(1) goes on to provide that: 'A carrier or carriage service provider must not engage in anticompetitive conduct.' section 151AJ(2) states:

> A carrier or carriage service provider engages in anti-competitive conduct if the carrier or carriage service provider:
>
> a. has a substantial degree of power in a market; and
> b. either:
>   - takes advantage of that power with the effect, or likely effect, of substantially lessening competition in that or any other telecommunications market; or
>   - takes advantage of that power, and engages in other conduct on one or more occasions, with the combined effect, or likely combined effect, of substantially lessening competition in that or any other telecommunications market.

These provisions apply in addition to the competition law provisions of Part IV of the CCA.

20. Further, section 151(AJ)(3) indicates that a carrier or carriage service provider engages in anticompetitive conduct if they engage in conduct in contravention of section 45 (collusive arrangements); section 45AJ (making a contract containing a cartel provision); section 45AK (giving effect to a cartel provision); section 46 (misuse of market power); section 47 (exclusive dealing) or section 48 (resale price maintenance). If the regulator is satisfied that there has been a breach of this specific legislation, it may issue a competition notice specifying the nature of the breach.[6] Once this notice has been issued, this is prima facie evidence that there is a breach of the competition rules, and the onus reverts to the carrier or the carriage

6. Section 151AKA(1) of the *Competition and Consumer Act 2010*.

service provider to establish otherwise.[7] The penalties include a pecuniary penalty of AUD 10 million (Aus), plus a continuing penalty of AUD 1 million/day. Injunctions and damages are also available.[8]

21. A further sector with specialist legislation applying to them is energy. Part IIIAA of the CCA creates the Australian Energy Regulator (AER) with responsibility for electricity regulation. This body is responsible for the economic regulation of the national energy market. The competition provisions of Part IV continue to apply to the energy sector. The reason behind the introduction of the AER was a view that competing energy sources should be regulated on competition principles rather than the ad-hoc and confusing approach that had developed on a state-by-state basis. The AER is an independent legal entity but operates as a part of the ACCC.[9] The AER is also responsible, except in the state of Western Australia, for the regulation of gas transmission and distribution networks.

§3. State-Owned Enterprises and Public Utilities

22. Section 2A(1) of the CCA provides that Part IV of the Act applies to the Crown in right of the Commonwealth insofar as the Commonwealth carries on business. The Crown cannot be liable for a pecuniary penalty or to be prosecuted, though this exemption does not apply to an authority of the Commonwealth[10] or someone with whom the Commonwealth transacts.[11] Similarly, the competition rules will apply to the state or territory Crown, insofar as they carry on business.[12] Part IV will also apply to a local government body to the extent that it carries on business.[13] Section 2C specifies that the following do not constitute the carrying on of a business:

(a) imposing or collecting:
  - taxes; or
  - levies; or
  - fees for licenses;

(b) the granting, revoking, suspension of licenses;
(c) transactions involving non-commercial activities of the Crown, or between Crown authorities; and
(d) the acquisition of primary products by a government body under legislative direction.

7. Section 151AN of the *Competition and Consumer Act 2010.*
8. See ss 151BX, 151CA & 151CC of the *Competition and Consumer Act 2010.*
9. Section 44AE of the *Competition and Consumer Act 2010.*
10. Section 2A(3A) of the *Competition and Consumer Act 2010.*
11. *Australian Competition and Consumer Commission v. Baxter Healthcare* (2007) 237 ALR 512. Competitive Neutrality is a critical aspect of the Australian Competition Law landscape. 2018, volume 25(3) of the *Competition and Consumer Law Journal* was dedicated to the consideration of this topic.
12. Section 2B(1) of the *Competition and Consumer Act 2010.*
13. Section 2BA of the *Competition and Consumer Act 2010.*

23. To determine the applicability of this part of the legislation, it is critical to ascertain whether the authority is a manifestation of the Crown. The Crown refers to the executive as distinct from the legislative arm of the government.[14] In Australia, there are ten manifestations of the Crown.[15] An example of the difficulties in determining whether a body is a manifestation of the Crown can be seen in the case of *NT Power Generation v. Power and Water Authority*.[16] The Power and Water Authority (PAWA (a statutory authority)) regulated and supplied electricity in the Northern Territory. NT Power Generation sought access to the infrastructure. PAWA argued that it was not carrying on a business in the provision of infrastructure services. This argument was accepted at both the trial judge and Full Federal Court level but was rejected by the High Court. Importantly the High Court considered that the impugned conduct does not need to be the actual business in which it was engaged. PAWA's decision was taken because of the impact it could have on its business, and, therefore, the denial of access was conduct that advanced its business activities.[17]

§4. Sensible Effect and *De Minimis*

24. In Australia, there is no widely used doctrine of sensible effect and *de minimis*.

14. *NT Power Generation v. Power and Water Authority* (2004) 219 90 CLR 90.
15. The Commonwealth, the six states (New South Wales, Victoria, Queensland, Tasmania, South Australia and Western Australia) and three territories (Australian Capital Territory, Northern Territory and Norfolk Island).
16. (2004) 219 CLR 90.
17. (2004) 219 CLR 90, [72].

Chapter 3. Overview of Substantive Provisions

§1. Restrictive Agreements

25. The two critical provisions for horizontal arrangements that lessen competition are section 45AA and section 45 of the CCA.

45AA: A corporation must not make, or give effect to, a contract, arrangement or understanding that contains a cartel provision.

26. A cartel provision is a provision relating to:

(a) price-fixing;
(b) restricting outputs in the production and supply chain;
(c) allocating customers, suppliers or territories; or
(d) bid-rigging;

by parties that are, or would otherwise be, in competition with each other.

27. Section 45 provides:

(1) A corporation must not:
  (a) make a contract or arrangement, or arrive at an understanding, if a provision of the proposed contract, arrangement or understanding has the purpose, or would have or be likely to have the effect, of substantially lessening competition;
  (b) give effect to a provision of a contract, arrangement or understanding, if that provision has the purpose, or has or is likely to have the effect, of substantially lessening competition; or
  (c) engage with one or more persons in a concerted practice that has the purpose, or has or is likely to have the effect, of substantially lessening competition.

Remedies[18] available for breach include the following:
For the ACCC:

- pecuniary penalties of up to the higher of AUD 10 million, three times the benefit obtained, or 10% of the annual turnover for a corporation and AUD 500,000 for an individual;
- injunctions; and
- ancillary orders;

18. Examples of the application of these remedies can be seen in *Australian Competition and Consumer Commission v. Thai Airways International Public Co Ltd* [2012] FCA 1434 and *Australian Competition and Consumer Commission v. Cathay Pacific Airways Ltd (No. 3)* [2012] FCA 1392.

Individuals may apply to the court for:

- injunctions;
- damages; and
- ancillary orders.

Corporations are entitled to seek authorization for a restrictive agreement under section 88 of the CCA.

28. Gaol Terms can also be sought for serious cases of collusive conduct: up to ten years gaol and/or fines of $420,000 (AUS) per criminal cartel offence (*see* Division 1, Part 4 CCA).

29. The underlying feature necessary to establish a breach is collusion. If business is able to demonstrate independent decision-making, there can be no collusion.

30. Key criteria in establishing a breach include whether:

- there is a contract, arrangement or understanding;
- that this has the requisite *purpose* or *effect*;
- that there is a *substantial lessening* of competition;
- in the *market.*

31. As can be seen, 'purpose' is critical within this provision, with this defined as follows:

> *Section 4F: (1) For the purposes of this Act*:
>
> a. a provision of a contract, arrangement or understanding or of a proposed contract, arrangement or understanding, or a covenant or a proposed covenant, shall be deemed to have had, or to have, a particular purpose if:
>   - the provision was included in the contract, arrangement or understanding or is to be included in the proposed contract, arrangement or understanding, and,
>   - that purpose was or is a substantial purpose; and
>
> b. a person shall be deemed to have engaged or to engage in conduct for a particular purpose or a particular reason if:
>   - the person engaged or engages in the conduct for purposes that included or include that purpose or for reasons that included or include that reason, as the case may be; and
>   - that purpose or reason was or is a substantial purpose or reason.

32. Other lesser-used provision dealing with restrictive agreements include:

(a) secondary boycotts for the purpose of causing substantial loss or damage (section 45D);

(b) secondary boycotts for the purpose of causing a substantial lessening of competition (section 45DA);
(c) boycotts affecting trade or commerce (section 45DB);
(d) involvement and liability of employee organizations (section 45DC); and
(e) situations in which boycotts are permitted (section 45DD).

§2. Dominant Undertakings

33. There is no prohibition against the possession of dominant power. Section 46 of the CCA provides that:

> 1. A corporation that has a substantial degree of power in a market must not engage in conduct that has the purpose, or has or likely to have the effect of substantially lessing competition in that market, or any other market in which the corporation or a body corporate related to that market, supplies or acquires goods or services.

The remedies, apart from gaol terms, are the same for a breach of section 46 as they were for section 45.

34. There are three fundamental points about section 46. These are:

- market power is not by itself a problem;
- market power can be legally used, provided that the market power is not used for the purpose or effect, or likely effect of substantially lessening competition;
- a corporation without market power can act to lessen competition. In other words, conduct that may be legitimate when the entity has no market power, becomes illegal when market power is obtained.

35. Section 46(3) allows the market power held by related corporate bodies to be aggregated in determining whether an entity has a substantial degree of power in a market. A related body corporate is defined by section 4A of the CCA. A body corporate will be deemed to the subsidiary of another body corporate if that other body corporate controls the composition of the board of directors or is in a position to cast more than half the votes at a general meeting or holds more than one-half of the allotted share capital. An illustration of related body corporate can be seen in *Australian Competition and Consumer Commission v. Rural Press Limited*,[19] where one company was a wholly owned subsidiary of another, much larger entity. They were related for the purposes of the CCA. A corporation can have market power, even though it may not substantially control the market, even though it does not have absolute freedom to act without constraint from competitors, and to avoid any doubt, more than one corporation may have a substantial degree of power in a market (section 46(3C)).

19. [2001] FCA 116.

36. The key focus of section 46 is the protection of competition, not of individual competitors.[20] The indicia of market power will include factor such as barriers to entry, the power to establish and control price, excess capacity, market share and vertical integration. Barriers to entry can arise from a vast array of factors, including legal constraints, physical constraints, technology, economies of scale, the capital requirements for a new entry or the capacity to block access. To establish a breach of section 46, the key factors that will need to be shown include:

- conduct by a corporation;
- that the conduct involves a market for goods or services in Australia;
- the corporation possessing a substantial degree of power in that market;
- and that the power was used for the purpose, or had the effect or likely effect of substantially lessening competition.

37. Section 46A replicates section 46, but with a focus on the trans-Tasman market between Australia and New Zealand.

38. As indicated, whilst there is no prohibition against having dominant power though Part IIIA of the *Competition and Consumer Act 1974* has provided a mechanism by which parties can seek access to facilities owned by another person. Declaration of access can occur by way of:

- declaration by the Minister following a recommendation by the NCC (with this being the most critical);
- certification of an industry-specific state or territory access regime; or
- an undertaking by the facility holder to the ACCC, setting out how access will be provided.

39. The declaration will set in place a process by which the conditions for access are mediated between the facility owner, the third party seeking access and the ACCC. Decisions may be appealed to the ACT. Section 44G(2) provides that declaration of a facility cannot occur unless:

(a) access or increased access will promote a material increase in competition;
(b) that it would be uneconomical to duplicate the facility;
(c) that the size of the facility is of national significance having regard to its size, its importance to trade or commerce or its importance to the national economy;
(d) that access can be granted without undue risk to health or safety;
(e) that access is not already subject to an effective access regime; and
(f) that access would not be contrary to the public interest.

40. Sectors, where access has been raised, include rail, shipping, energy, airports and water.[21]

---

20. *Queensland Wire Industries Pty Ltd v. Broken Hill Proprietary Co Ltd* (1989) 167 CLR 177, 192.
21. See S.G. Corones, *Competition Law in Australia*, 6th edn (Thomson Reuters, 2014), Ch. 14 for a discussion of these sectors.

§3. CONCENTRATIONS

41. Section 50 prohibits a person from acquiring, directly or indirectly, equity in a company or the assets of a person, if that acquisition would have the effect or be likely to have the effect of substantially lessening competition in a substantial market. The precise wording is as follows:

> Section 50(1): A corporation must not directly or indirectly:
>
> (a) acquire shares in the capital of a body corporate; or
> (b) acquire any assets of a person.
>
> If the acquisition would have the effect, or be likely to have the effect, of substantially lessening competition in a market.[22]

42. In considering this, it must have regard to the list of facts detailed in section 50(3).

(a) the actual and potential level of import competition in the market;
(b) the height of barriers to entry to the market;
(c) the level of concentration in the market;
(d) the degree of countervailing power in the market;
(e) the likelihood that the acquisition would result in the acquirer being able to significantly and sustainably increase prices or profit margins;
(f) the extent to which substitutes are available in the market or are likely to be available in the market;
(g) the dynamic characteristics of the market, including growth, innovation and product differentiation;
(h) the likelihood that the acquisition would result in the removal from the market of a vigorous and effective competitor; and
(i) the nature and extent of vertical integration in the market.

43. In addition to the remedies noted above, the ACCC, as well as individuals, can apply for divestiture as a remedial option.

44. Authorization immunity is available for section 50 acquisitions under section 88 of the CCA.

45. Section 50 looks directly at changes to market structure and the effect or likely effect such changes have on competition in a market. The other provisions of Part IV focus on market conduct. To establish a breach, it is necessary to define a market and isolate whether this will substantially lessen competition in that market. The width of the market as defined is critical to section 50 litigation. The broader the market, the less likely there will be a substantial lessening of competition; the more narrow the market, the greater likelihood of breach.

22. Section 50 relates to substantial markets for goods and services in Australia (s. 50(6)).

46. Under section 50, whatever the relevant market might be conceptually, it must be 'substantial' in either quantitative or qualitative terms. There is no definition in the legislation as to what 'substantial' means in this context. A market involving a small amount of turnover may still be substantial, where it can be shown that it is of such importance as to be qualitatively substantial within a community. Section 50A allows for the examination of acquisitions or mergers which take place outside Australia, but which have the effect, or likely effect, of substantially lessening competition in a market in Australia. The Merger Guidelines heavily influence merger regulation and litigation.

§4. OTHER PROHIBITIONS

47. Two other prohibitions complete the Part IV protections. They are:

- section 47 (exclusive dealing); and
- section 48 (resale price maintenance).

48. Section 47 of the CCA is an extraordinarily detailed provision that has, as its aim, a prohibition against suppliers limiting the freedom of buyers to buy from or to sell to whom they choose. Similarly, buyers are prevented, for the most part, from imposing restrictions on the freedom of suppliers to sell as they wish. These practices, known as exclusive dealing or occasionally, full-line forcing, are illegal under section 47 if they have the purpose, effect or likely effect of substantially lessening competition.

49. Remedies are as noted above.

50. Notification immunity (as distinct from authorization) under section 93 of the legislation is available for section 47 exclusive dealing practices.

51. Section 45 and section 47 of the CCA are generally seen to have some critical differences. Section 45 addresses what are commonly known as horizontal arrangements[23] between competitors at the same functional level. By contrast, section 47 is sent to address vertical arrangements that may exist between retailer and wholesaler or wholesaler and manufacturer. Section 47 also does not speak in terms of contracts, arrangements or understandings as does section 45, but rather in terms of the conditional acquisition or supply of goods or services.

52. Where arrangements could breach both sections 45 and 47, the conduct is to be considered under section 47 (section 45(6)).

23. However, it should be noted that the High Court of Australia disapproved of the use of the terms 'horizontal' and 'vertical' arrangements. *Visy Paper Pty Ltd v. Australian Competition and Consumer Commission* (2003) 201 ALR 414.

53. Section 47 lists exhaustively the different vertical restraint practices that, if they have the purpose, effect or likely effect of substantially lessening competition, are illegal. However, its underlying theme is, as with much of the competition law, that prohibitions or restrictions, which prevent businesses from maximizing their own welfare, are illegal.

54. Section 48 prohibits the practice of resale price maintenance. What this means is that a supplier of goods or services cannot dictate to the next person in the functional chain how those goods or services will be sold. Again, its policy focus is in allowing individual businesses the freedom to set their own pricing structure without interference from others in the chain of supply. For this reason, resale price maintenance is also known as vertical price-fixing. A recommended price will not see a breach of the legislation where the retailer is able to ignore this recommendation (section 97).

55. A supplier will engage in resale price maintenance (*see* section 96) if they:

- make it known that goods will not be supplied unless they are sold at a specific price;
- provides some inducement for goods not to be sold at a price other than dictated by the supplier;
- enters into an agreement that will fix the prices;
- withholds goods because the retailer or third party has not agreed to sell at a certain price; or
- uses in relation to goods a statement indicating the price that the goods are to be sold.

56. Resale price maintenance contains a specific defence of a loss leader. The loss leader defence (section 98) allows the withholding of supply, where in the year preceding the withholding of supply, the person seeking supply has used the goods of the supplier as a means to attract customers to that business, or otherwise promoting the business of that person. The defence will not apply where there is a genuine clearance or seasonal sale (section 98(3)).

57. Remedies are as noted above.

58. Notification immunity is available for section 48 resale price maintenance under section 93.

§5. Tests of Illegality

I. Per Se Prohibitions and Naked Restraints

59. As can be seen from the preceding discussion, most provisions rely on the establishment of a substantial lessening of competition; resale price maintenance is per se illegal. The Cartel provisions rely on detailed meeting of a purpose/effect provision *and* the requirement that the parties are in competition with each other. The provisions are as follows:

> (45AD)For the purposes of this Act, a provision of a contract, arrangement or understanding is a ***cartel provision*** if:
>
> (a) either of the following conditions is satisfied in relation to the provision:
>   (i) the purpose/effect condition set out in subsection(2);
>   (ii) the purpose condition set out in subsection(3); and
> (b) the competition condition set out in subsection(4) is satisfied in relation to the provision.
>
> Purpose/effect condition
>
> (2) The purpose/effect condition is satisfied if the provision has the purpose, or has or is likely to have the effect, of directly or indirectly:
>   (a) fixing, controlling or maintaining; or
>   (b) providing for the fixing, controlling or maintaining of;
>   the price for, or a discount, allowance, rebate or credit in relation to;
>   (c) goods or services supplied, or likely to be supplied, by any or all of the parties to the contract, arrangement or understanding; or
>   (d) goods or services acquired, or likely to be acquired, by any or all of the parties to the contract, arrangement or understanding; or
>   (e) goods or services re-supplied, or likely to be re-supplied, by persons or classes of persons to whom those goods or services were supplied by any or all of the parties to the contract, arrangement or understanding; or
>   (f) goods or services likely to be re-supplied by persons or classes of persons to whom those goods or services are likely to be supplied by any or all of the parties to the contract, arrangement or understanding.
>
> Note 1: The purpose/effect condition can be satisfied when a provision is considered with related provisions – see subsection(8).
> Note 2: ***Party*** has an extended meaning – see section 45AC.
>
> Purpose condition
>
> (3) The purpose condition is satisfied if the provision has the purpose of directly or indirectly:
>   (a) preventing, restricting or limiting:
>   (i) the production, or likely production, of goods by any or all of the parties to the contract, arrangement or understanding; or
>   (ii) the capacity, or likely capacity, of any or all of the parties to the contract, arrangement or understanding to supply services; or
>   (iii) the supply, or likely supply, of goods or services to persons or classes of persons by any or all of the parties to the contract, arrangement or understanding; or

(iv) the acquisition, or likely acquisition, of goods or services from persons or classes of persons by any or all of the parties to the contract, arrangement or understanding; or

(b) allocating between any or all of the parties to the contract, arrangement or understanding:

(i) the persons or classes of persons who have acquired, or who are likely to acquire, goods or services from any or all of the parties to the contract, arrangement or understanding; or

(ii) the persons or classes of persons who have supplied, or who are likely to supply, goods or services to any or all of the parties to the contract, arrangement or understanding; or

(iii) the geographical areas in which goods or services are supplied, or likely to be supplied, by any or all of the parties to the contract, arrangement or understanding; or

(iv) the geographical areas in which goods or services are acquired, or likely to be acquired, by any or all of the parties to the contract, arrangement or understanding; or

(c) ensuring that in the event of a request for bids in relation to the supply or acquisition of goods or services:

(i) one or more parties to the contract, arrangement or understanding bid, but one or more other parties do not; or

(ii) 2 or more parties to the contract, arrangement or understanding bid, but at least 2 of them do so on the basis that one of those bids is more likely to be successful than the others; or

(iii) 2 or more parties to the contract, arrangement or understanding bid, but not all of those parties proceed with their bids until the suspension or finalization of the request for bids process; or

(iv) 2 or more parties to the contract, arrangement or understanding bid and proceed with their bids, but at least 2 of them proceed with their bids on the basis that one of those bids is more likely to be successful than the others; or

(v) 2 or more parties to the contract, arrangement or understanding bid, but a material component of at least one of those bids is worked out in accordance with the contract, arrangement or understanding

Note 1: For example, subparagraph(3)(a)(iii) will not apply in relation to a roster for the supply of after-hours medical services if the roster does not prevent, restrict or limit the supply of services.
Note 2: The purpose condition can be satisfied when a provision is considered with related provisions – see subsection (9).
Note 3: ***Party*** has an extended meaning – see section 45AC.

Competition condition

(4) The competition condition is satisfied if at least 2 of the parties to the contract, arrangement or understanding:

(a) are or are likely to be; or

(b) but for any contract, arrangement or understanding would be or would be likely to be;

in competition with each other in relation to … .

II. Balancing Tests

60. Where the conduct is only illegal where there is a substantial lessening of competition, the courts are required to determine the market, and then consider the extent to which this involves a lessening of competition. It is some features similar to the US rule of reason test. Applications for authorization and notification involve a balancing exercise whereby the party seeking authorization is required to show that the benefit to the public by the anticompetitive arrangements outweighs the detriment to the public caused by the lessening of competition (*see*, for example, section 90(7)), or there is no substantial lessening of competition. Public detriment is not defined in the legislation but has been given a broad meaning encompassing any impairment to the community generally.[24] What happens as a matter of practice is a comparison of the position with the authorization, and one without. As with public detriment, public benefit has not been defined by the legislature. However, a vast array of matters have been accepted as being of benefit to the public. These have included economic as well as non-economic matters such as the promotion of sport,[25] the promotion of breast-feeding,[26] environmental considerations[27] and an increase in public safety.[28]

III. Merger Tests

61. Mergers are prohibited if they result in a substantial lessening of competition. In determining whether there has been a substantial lessening of competition, the ACCC examines this from the perspective of one to two years ahead. What will the market look like with the merger? What will it look like without the merger? Under section 50(3) of the CCA, a range of factors must be taken into account to decide whether a merger will affect competition. These include:

- the level of import competition;
- barriers to entry;
- concentration in the market;
- degree of countervailing power;
- the capacity to increase prices post-merger;
- substitutes in the market;
- dynamic characteristics of the market;

24. *Re 2-Eleven Stores Pty Ltd* [1994] ATPR 42, 644 (41–357).
25. *Speedo Knitting Mills* [1981] ATPR (Com) 50–016.
26. *Abott Australia* [1992] ATPR (Com) 50–123.
27. *Association of Fluorocarbon Consumers and Manufacturers* [1994] ATPR (Com) 50–153.
28. *Australian Tyre Dealers' and Retreaders' Association* [1994] ATPR (Com) 50–162.

– the likelihood of a vigorous competitor being removed from the market; and
– the extent of vertical integration in the market.

Chapter 4. Overview of Main Notions

§1. Undertaking

62. The word 'undertaking' is not a key notion used within Australian Competition Law.

§2. Relevant Market

63. As noted above, there are different tests to determine whether a business practice is anticompetitive . Some aspects, such as price-fixing, are currently per se illegal. By contrast, section 46 relies upon misuse of market power test.

64. Substantial lessening of competition and a substantial degree of market power both require the identification of a relevant market, whereas the per se offence of resale price maintenance does not.

I. Market

65. In Australia, the notion of a market is essentially based upon economic criteria. The key features of the economic base behind the definition of market are as follows:

- competition within the market is not a static situation;
- to be in a competitive market no one seller or buyer has the power to establish a price of the product; and
- barriers to entry in a competitive marketplace are low.[29]

Section 4E of the CCA defines a market in the following manner:

> 'market' means a market in Australia and, when used in relation to any goods or services, includes a market for those goods or services and other goods or services that are substitutable for, or otherwise competitive with, the first-mentioned goods or services.

66. This definition was elaborated upon in *Queensland Co-operative Milling Association Ltd/Defiance Holdings Ltd, Re Proposed Merger with Barnes Milling Ltd*[30] where it was stated: '[A] market is the field of actual and potential transactions between buyers and sellers amongst whom there can be strong substitution, at least in the long run, if given a sufficient price incentive.' In *Australian Competition*

29. *Re Queensland Co-op Milling Assn Ltd and Defiance Holdings Ltd* (1976) 8 ALR 481; 25 FLR 169; ATPR para. 40-012.
30. (1976) ATPR para. 40-012 at 17-247.

and Consumer Commission v Flight Centre Travel Group Ltd,[31] the High Court considered that the existence of a market is determined by the extent of the substitutability of the goods or services. Accordingly, a travel agent was in competition with international airlines for the supply of international airline tickets, as the tickets from either were substitutable with each other.

67. Also, the analysis of the competitive process cannot be divorced from commercial reality. Conduct occurred in a market in Australia even though the two international airlines had engaged in price-fixing in relation to air cargo surcharges from the ports of Hong Kong, Singapore and Indonesia to destinations in Australia. The place where the collusive behaviour was signed does not say anything significant about the location of the rivalrous behaviour for the purposes of section 4E.[32]

68. A market has four dimensions. These are product, geographical, functional and, in some cases, time. The significance of market definition was identified in *Queensland Wire Industries v. BHP*[33] where it was stated:

> After identifying the appropriate product level, it is necessary to describe accurately the parameters of the market in which the defendant's product competes: too narrow a description of the market will create the appearance of more market power than in fact exists; too broad a description will create the appearance of less market power than there is.

69. The product market requires the identification of the relevant goods or services under examination. The geographic dimensions of the market require the parties to determine the extent to which a willing buyer will travel to purchase the product. The functional analysis of determining the relevant market requires the consideration of whether the party under examination is at the manufacturing level, wholesale or retail. The time dimension of the market necessitates consideration of whether the examination should be in the medium to a long run or, because of the specific nature of the good or service, that short-run examination is required.[34] In establishing the market boundaries, the parties will examine what goods or services are substitutable for the goods or services under question. This test of substitution will establish the area of close competition between firms in the marketplace.[35] The extent to which one good or service may be substituted for another is determined by the cross elasticity of dimension and supply.[36] The reason for undertaking this sort of examination is to determine what the changes in consumption or production will occur if the business offers a less attractive option. Cross elasticity of demand and supply, while informative, will not identify the market on its own. Market analysis

31. (2016) 261 CLR 203.
32. *Air New Zealand v Australian Competition and Consumer Commission; PT Garuda Indonesia Ltd v Australian Competition and Consumer Commission* (2017) 91 ALJR 648.
33. (1989) ATPR para. 40-928 at 50-008.
34. See generally, *Re Tooth & Co Ltd and Tooheys Ltd* (1979) 39 FLR 1, 38–39.
35. *Queensland Wire Industries Pty Ltd v. Broken Hill Proprietary Co Ltd* (1989) 167 CLR 177, 188.
36. *Queensland Wire Industries Pty Ltd v. Broken Hill Proprietary Co Ltd* (1989) 167 CLR 177, 199.

is not solely an economic analysis and does involve the making of value judgments.[37] Relevant considerations in determining the market include the following:

- the behaviour of consumers;[38]
- the focus will be on practical and feasible substitutes rather than those that may exist at the hypothetical level;[39]
- it is not strictly necessary that each product be within the same market for precisely the same function;[40]
- single brand markets while possible will be rare;[41] and
- survey evidence of market behaviour is permissible in determining the boundaries of a market.[42]

§3. Market Power/Dominant Position

70. Through section 46 of the CCA, a corporation with a substantial degree of market power is prohibited from engaging in conduct that has the purpose, or has or is likely to have the effect of substantially lessening competition in that market. Obviously closely linked to the definition of market, market power is the capacity of a company to behave in a way that is different from that of an entity in a competitive market. In other words, market power is the ability to raise prices and reduce output without affecting consumer behaviour. The degree to which the company can increase prices profitably without losing customers to other competitors represents the measure of its market power. Obviously two or more companies acting in concert can enjoy this type of market power.

71. However, it is important to remember that the successful corporation is able through the competitive process to gain market power. It is only the effect or purpose of this power that is of concern to the competition laws. In this sense, increasing market power may represent the result of exceptional corporate results. It is not necessary that the business be dominant to enjoy market power.[43] The key concept in determining whether a corporation has market power is whether it is free to act

37. *Queensland Wire Industries Pty Ltd v. Broken Hill Proprietary Co Ltd* (1989) 167 CLR 177, 195–196.
38. *Arnotts Ltd v. Trade Practices Commission* (1990) 24 FCR 313.
39. *Australia Meat Holdings Pty Ltd v. Trade Practices Commission* (1989) ATPR paras 40-923, 50-091.
40. *Arnotts Ltd v. Trade Practices Commission* (1990) 24 FCR 313.
41. *Mark Lyons Pty Ltd v. Bursill Sportsgear Pty Ltd* (1987) 75 ALR 581.
42. *Arnotts Ltd v. Trade Practices Commission* (1990) 24 FCR 313. The Federal Court of Australia has issued practice note no. 11 that details the requirements that a survey must meet before it is given any significant weight.
43. *Australian Competition and Consumer Commission v. Australian Safeway Stores Pty Ltd* (2003) 129 FCR 339.

without competitive constraints on its behaviour.[44] Market power can also exist in circumstances where there is only one dominant buyer, this is known as monopsony (in contrast to a monopoly).

72. In determining whether there is market power, the cases have analysed a number of factors. These include:

- the extent of barriers to entry to the market;[45]
- the extent to which the corporation can change its behaviour without affecting its customer base;[46]
- the strategic behaviour of the corporation;[47] and
- the market share of the corporation.[48]

§4. Agreements and Concerted Practices

73. The key in establishing a breach of the collusive provisions of the anti-competition laws of Australia (sections 45AA and 45) is that there is a contract, arrangement or understanding. Contract, arrangement or understanding is not defined in the legislation. There is no doubt, however, that agreements that do not meet legal requirements for a valid contract can still be caught by the operation of this provision. Nevertheless, it is the cases to which recourse must be had to determine the meaning of contract, arrangement or understanding.

I. Contract

74. Normal contractual principles will apply.

II. Arrangement

75. The typical starting point in determining the meaning of this is to follow the words of Diplock J. in *Re British Basic Slag:*[49]

> is not a term of art … it involves a meeting of the minds between two or more persons and it involves mutuality in that each party assuming he is a reasonable and conscientious man would regard himself as being in some degree under a duty whether moral or legal to conduct himself in a particular way as

44. *Boral Besser Masonry Ltd v. Australian Competition and Consumer Commission* (2003) 215 CLR 374; *Australian Competition and Consumer Commission v. Australian Safeway Stores Pty Ltd* (2003) 129 FCR 339.
45. *Queensland Wire Industries Pty Ltd v. Broken Hill Proprietary Co Ltd* (1989) 167 CLR 177.
46. *Queensland Wire Industries Pty Ltd v. Broken Hill Proprietary Co Ltd* (1989) 167 CLR 177.
47. *Queensland Wire Industries Pty Ltd v. Broken Hill Proprietary Co Ltd* (1989) 167 CLR 177.
48. *Queensland Wire Industries Pty Ltd v. Broken Hill Proprietary Co Ltd* (1989) 167 CLR 177.
49. [1963] 2 All ER 807, 819.

> the case may be at any rate so long as the other party or parties conducted themselves in the way contemplated by the arrangement.

76. This statement has been followed in Australia.[50] In summary, the elements of an arrangement appear to be:

- a meeting of minds by some form of communication;
- the creation of expectations in the minds of the parties; and
- the acceptance that each party will act in a particular way.[51]

77. Consensus is required, and an assumption that people will act in a certain way.[52]

III. Understanding

78. An understanding is something less than a binding contract.[53] In *Top Performance Motors Pty Ltd v. Ira Berk (Qld) Pty* Ltd[54] Smithers J. stated:

> It seems to me also that an understanding must involve the meeting of two or more minds. Where the minds of the parties are at one that a proposed transaction between them proceeds on the basis of the maintenance of a particular state of affairs or the adoption of a particular course of conduct, it would seem that there would be an understanding within the meaning of the Act.

79. Whilst, it is recognized that it is a broad and flexible notion, there is recognition that it must be a consensual dealing between the parties and involve a meeting of minds.[55] A mere hope or expectation that people will act in a particular way is insufficient to qualify as an understanding.[56] As to whether mutuality in the sense of a mutual commitment is still a matter open to debate. The suggestion from the cases is that it is not.[57] An understanding is possibly less formal than an arrangement.[58]

---

50. *Australian Competition and Consumer Commission v. Universal Music Australia Pty Ltd* (2003) 131 FCR 529. It was noted in *Australian Competition and Consumer Commission v. Leahy Petroleum Pty Ltd* [2007] FCA 794, [26] that 'In general, [an arrangement] appears to connote a consensual dealing lacking some of the essential elements that would otherwise make it a contract.'
51. *Australian Competition and Consumer Commission v. Leahy Petroleum Pty Ltd* [2007] FCA 794.
52. *Trade Practices Commission v. Email Ltd* (1980) 31 ALR 53.
53. *Australian Competition and Consumer Commission v. Leahy Petroleum Pty Ltd* [2007] FCA 794.
54. *Top Performance Motors Pty Ltd v. Ira Berk (Qld) Pty* Ltd (1975) 24 FLR 286 at 291.
55. *Australian Competition and Consumer Commission v. Leahy Petroleum Pty Ltd* [2007] FCA 794.
56. *Apco Service Stations Pty Ltd v. Australian Competition and Consumer Commission* [2005] ATPR 42-078.
57. *Australian Competition and Consumer Commission v. Leahy Petroleum Pty Ltd* (2004) ATPR (Digest) para. 46-260.
58. *Australian Competition and Consumer Commission v. Australian Medical Assn Western Australia Branch Inc* (2003) 199 ALR 423.

§5. RESTRICTION OF COMPETITION

80. Where the conduct requires a restriction of competition to be a breach, the Australian regulator will be required to show that there has been; either, the purpose, effect or likely effect of a substantial lessening of competition. Competition is currently defined in the legislation as follows:

(a) competition from goods that are, or are capable of being, imported into Australia; and
(b) competition from services that are rendered, or are capable of being rendered, in Australia by persons not resident or not carrying on business in Australia.

81. Lessening of competition is also defined:

> For the purposes of this Act, references to the lessening of competition shall be read as including references to preventing or hindering competition.[59]

82. However, there is no definition of 'substantial'. Case law has provided little guidance. It has been indicated that substantial must mean something in a sense of considerable as opposed to being insignificant or minimal.[60] It is an imprecise phrase susceptible to ambiguity.[61] For example, it has described in the following way:

> [S]ubstantial … can, in an appropriate context, mean real or of substance as distinct from ephemeral or nominal. It can mean large, weighty, or big. It can be used in a relative sense or can indicate an absolute significance, quantity or size.[62]

83. In ascertaining whether conduct has the effect of substantially lessening competition, the court will make both a qualitative and quantitative assessment of the impact of the conduct.[63] Critical will be determining whether the change is substantial in that it would be incompatible with a competitive outcome in that particular market.[64] The structure of the market will be considered, with this being done over the long-term.[65] Conduct will likely have the effect of substantially lessening competition if there is a real possibility that this will occur.[66] Conduct will have the purpose of substantially lessening competition where that is the subjective purpose of those engaging in particular conduct.[67]

59. Section 4G *Competition and Consumer Act 2010.*
60. *ASX Operations v. Pont Data Australia Pty Ltd (No. 1)* (1990) 27 FCR 460, 478.
61. *Radio 2UE Sydney Pty Ltd v. Stereo FM Pty Ltd* (1982) 44 ALR 557.
62. *Tillmanns Butcheries Pty Ltd v. Australasian Meat Industry Employees' Union* (1979) 27 ALR 367.
63. *Dandy Power Equipment Pty Ltd v. Mercury Marine Pty Ltd* (1982) 44 ALR 173.
64. *Eastern Express Pty Ltd v. General Newspapers Pty Ltd* (1991) 30 FCR 385.
65. *Australian Gas Light Co v. Australian Competition and Consumer Commission (No. 3)* (2003) 137 FCR 317.
66. *Tillmanns Butcheries Pty Ltd v. Australasian Meat Industry Employees' Union* (1979) 27 ALR 367.
67. *News Ltd v. South Sydney District Rugby League Football Club Ltd* (2003) 215 CLR 563.

§6. Monopolization and Abuse of Dominance

84. Section 46 of the CCA provides that a company with a substantial degree of power in a market shall not engage in conduct that has the purpose, or has or is likely to have the effect of substantially lessening competition.

I. Definitions Associated with Section 46

85. Many of the definitions relevant to section 46 have already been discussed. These include corporation, market, market power, substantial lessening of competition, and purpose.

§7. Concentrations

I. Definitions Associated with Section 50

86. The three elements needed to find a breach of section 50 are as follows:

- a corporation;
- acquiring directly or indirectly shares in assets in a corporation/body corporate; and
- the effect or likely effect of substantially lessening competition in the markets.

87. Corporation has been previously discussed, as has substantial lessening of competition. The term asset is not defined but is likely to be read widely. Acquire is defined by section 4(4) of the Act. This states:

> a. a reference to the acquisition of shares in the capital of a company of a body corporate shall be construed as a reference to an acquisition, whether alone or jointly with another person, or any legal or equitable interest in such shares; and
> b. a reference to the acquisition of assets of a person shall be construed as a reference to an acquisition, whether alone or jointly with another person, of any legal or equitable interest in such assets but does not include a reference to an acquisition by way of charge only or an acquisition in the ordinary course of business.

88. The correct interpretation of 'directly or indirectly' is a matter of some debate. Some view an indirect acquisition as relating to the use of an agent or trustee of nominee of the acquiring company.[68] A second opinion is that indirectly should

68. *Trade Practices Commission v. Australian Iron & Steel Pty Ltd* (1990) 22 FCR 305.

be read widely to cover all types of indirect acquisitions, including where assets are acquired through a wholly owned subsidiary.[69] In the context of section 50, market is interpreted to mean:

> 50(6) market means a substantial market for goods or services in:
>
> a. Australia; or
> b. a State; or
> c. a Territory; or
> d. a region of Australia.

89. Some guidance is provided by the *Merger Guidelines,* which indicate that while a market may be small on a national level, the specific market may well be considered substantial when examining the matter from a state or regional level. Further, where the product is essential, but only a small component of the final product, it may still be considered substantial for the purposes of this part of the legislation.[70]

90. It is unusual for the regulator to commence proceedings in relation to section 50 matters. More likely is that the parties will approach the ACCC on a formal or informal basis to identify any concerns that may be had in relation to the proposed acquisition. In considering the matter, the ACCC will follow a five-stage process:

- identify the market;
- consider market concentration;
- the next step is to consider import competition;
- an examination of the barriers to entry, including legal and regulatory barriers, costs, economies of scale, brand loyalty and the threat of a strategic response by the other participants in the market; and
- any other structural or conduct matters.

91. If a person outside of Australia acquires a controlling interest in a body corporate and by that, acquires controlling interest of a corporation in Australia that has the effect, or is likely to have effect of substantially lessening competition, the ACT may make a declaration.[71] The effect of this declaration is that the corporation in Australia must not so long as the declaration remains in force carry on business in the market to which the declaration relates.[72]

---

69. *Australian Meat Holdings Pty Ltd v. Trade Practices Commission* (1989) ATPR para. 40-932.
70. ACCC, *Merger Guidelines,* [5.82]–[5.86].
71. Section 50A *Competition and Consumer Act Competition and Consumer Act 2010.*
72. Section 50A(6) *Competition and Consumer Act Competition and Consumer Act 2010.*

§8. JOINT VENTURES

92. Whilst joint ventures have no commonly understood common law meaning in Australia, the term is defined for the purposes of the CCA. Section 4J states as follows:

> In this Act:
>
> a. a reference to a joint venture is reference to an activity in trade or commerce:
>   - carried on jointly by two or more persons, whether or not in partnership; or
>   - carried on by a body corporate formed by two or more persons for the purpose of enabling those persons to carry on that activity jointly by means of their joint control, or by means of their ownership of shares in the capital, of that body corporate; and
>
> b. a reference to a contract or arrangement made or understanding arrived at, or to a proposed contract or arrangement to be made or proposed understanding to be arrived at, for the purposes of a joint venture shall, in relation to a joint venture by way of an activity carried on by a body corporate as mentioned in subparagraph (a)(ii), be read as including a reference to the memorandum and articles of association, rules or other document that constitute or constitutes, or are or is to constitute, that body corporate.

93. Further provisions dealing with joint ventures in the legislation include section 45AO and 45AP of the CCA, *which* provides a defence for joint venture participants to an allegation that the arrangements breach the cartel provisions. To use the defence, it is necessary to find that the provision is for the purposes of a joint venture, reasonably necessary for undertaking the joint venture, the joint venture is for the production of goods, supply of goods or services or the acquisition of goods or services, and does not have the purpose of substantially lessening competition.

Chapter 5. Consequences of Violations and Enforcement Institutions

§1. Administrative Enforcement

I. The Antitrust Authorities

94. In Australia, the ACCC is the national agency that deals with competition and antitrust matters. The ACCC has responsibility for enforcing the CCA and the state/territory application legislation.

Under section 6A(2) of the CCA, the ACCC:

- is a body corporate, with perpetual succession;
- has an official seal;
- may acquire, hold and dispose of real and personal property; and
- may sue or be sued in its corporate name.

95. The ACCC encourages vigorous competition and fair trade in the market place to benefit consumers, business and the community. It also regulates national infrastructure industries. Its primary responsibility is to ensure that individuals and businesses comply with Australia's Federal competition, fair trading and consumer protection laws.

A. *Formation and Composition*

96. The ACCC was established in 1995 with the amalgamation of its predecessor, the Australian Trade Practices Commission (TPC) and the Prices Surveillance Authority (PSA). The ACCC is an independent statutory authority. The ACCC has a chairperson, deputy chairs, full-time members, ex officio, and associate members. Appointments to the ACCC involve participation by Federal, state and territory governments. The terms and conditions of appointment are established by the Governor-General pursuant to section 8 of the CCA. The period of office does not exceed five years. Commissioners are eligible for reappointment. The ACCC members are collectively referred to as the Commission. The ACCC's business is conducted through formal meetings and the Commission meets regularly, usually weekly, to make decisions on matters investigated by the ACCC. The meetings are usually chaired by the chairperson and must include at least two of the full-time members. Matters include:

- mergers;
- authorizations;
- notifications;
- whether to begin court proceedings; and
- decisions about access to infrastructure facilities.

B. Investigating Powers

97. Traditionally, to investigate and enforce the Act the ACCC has relied upon section 155(1) of the CCA to compel production of information, documents or evidence where the ACCC, the Chairperson or Deputy Chairperson has 'reason to believe' that a person is capable of furnishing information, producing documents or giving evidence relating to a matter that constitutes, or may constitute, a contravention of the Act.

98. Failure to comply or knowingly furnishing information or giving evidence that is false or misleading risks punishment of a fine or up to twelve months imprisonment.

99. The ACCC also has search and seizure powers under Part XID of the CCA, which enable it to enter premises:

- by consent; or
- under a search warrant issued by a magistrate.

100. The ACCC has a number of investigatory powers at its disposal.

101. It has the power to issue a notice requiring a person or company to provide documents, information and/or to give evidence under oath where it believes that person is capable of furnishing information, producing documents or giving evidence relating to a matter that constitutes, or may constitute, a contravention of the CCA.[73]

102. The ACCC also has the power to seek a search warrant from a magistrate[74] and can also obtain documents pursuant to the issue of a subpoena.

C. Adjudicating Powers (Ascertaining and Sanctioning)

103. A grant of authorization in respect of particular conduct allows the applicant and others involved in that conduct to proceed with the conduct with immunity from further proceedings under the CCA.[75] The ACCC has the power to grant authorization[76] of certain types of conduct that would normally be prohibited by

73. Section 155 *Competition and Consumer Act Competition and Consumer Act 2010*. See also ACCC, *Section 155 of the Competition and Consumer Act* (March 2008).
74. Part XI *Competition and Consumer Act 2010*.
75. Part VII Div 1 (and Div 3 in the case of mergers) of the *Competition and Consumer Act 2010* contains the provisions relating to authorization.
76. The power to grant authorization is outlined in s. 88.

Part IV the CCA.[77] However, the ACCC has no power to grant authorization in respect of prior conduct (section 88(6)).[78]

104. The authorization test is set out in sections 90(7), which state that the conduct may not be authorized by the ACCC unless it is satisfied that the conduct:

- would result, or be likely to result;
- in a benefit to the public;
- which would outweigh the detriment to the public constituted by any lessening of competition that would result or be likely to result if the conduct were to take place:
- alternately, authorization can be granted if the conduct would not have the effect, or be likely to have the effect of substantially lessening competition.

105. The public benefit test, therefore, involves an assessment of:

- public benefits resulting from the conduct;
- any anticompetitive effect which it has; and
- the weighing up of these two elements.

106. Notification is a process under which parties may obtain immunity from legal action under the CCA if the conduct is in the public interest. Notification is only available for conduct involving:

- exclusive dealing;
- resale price maintenance (section 93); and
- collective bargaining (section 93).

107. The ACCC will assess the notification in accordance with the test if whether the conduct has the effect, or is likely to have the effect of substantially lessening competition, or where the benefit the public to the public will outweigh

77. Authorization may be sought for the following types of conduct:

- the making of, or giving effect to, a contract, arrangement or understanding which has a substantially anticompetitive effect (s. 88(1));
- the making of, or giving effect to, exclusionary provisions (s. 88(1));
- price-fixing arrangements involving goods or services (s. 88(1));
- covenants which have a substantially anticompetitive effect (s. 88(5));
- secondary boycotts and arrangements affecting the supply or acquisition of goods and falling within s. 45D, 45DA or 45DB (s. 88(7)) or s. 45E or 45EA (s. 88(7A));
- exclusive dealing (s. 88(8));
- resale price maintenance (s. 88(8A));
- mergers and acquisitions (s. 88(9) and s. 95AA–95AZN) – although application for authorization of mergers is dealt with by the Australian Competition Tribunal.

78. Conduct involving misuse of market power *may not* be authorized.

the cost. Notifications can only be lodged by the party engaging in exclusive dealing conduct. Notification notices must be in the prescribed form and accompanied by the prescribed fee.[79]

108. Notification provides immunity from legal proceedings from the date on which the details are validly lodged with the ACCC. The ACCC will remove immunity if it is satisfied that the notified conduct will result in a substantial lessening of competition and the public benefit that may result from the notified conduct will not outweigh the detriment to the public caused by the lessening of competition (*see* section 93(3)). The ACCC may remove the immunity, after issuing a draft notice outlining the reasons why it proposes to deny immunity. After considering submissions from interested parties in response to the draft notice and conducting its own investigations, the ACCC must decide whether to issue a final notice.

109. The ACCC's decision to remove immunity is reviewable. Where immunity is revoked, the notifying party cannot give a further notice in relation to the same or similar conduct.

110. Collective bargaining, an arrangement under which two or more competitors in an industry come together to negotiate terms and conditions with a supplier or customer, runs the risk of contravening section 45 or section 45AA of the CCA.

111. A notification procedure for collective bargaining arrangements for small businesses was introduced, with effect from 1 January 2007 (*see* section 93AB).

112. Three requirements must be satisfied in a collective bargaining notification:

1. the corporation must have made, or proposed to make, the initial contract with one or more persons about the supply of goods or services to, or the acquisition of particular goods or services from, another person (referred to as the target): section 93AB(2);
2. the corporation must reasonably expect that it will make one or more contracts with the target about the supply of one or more of those goods or services to, or the acquisition of one or more of those goods or services from, the target by the corporation: section 93AB(3);
3. the corporation must reasonably expect that the price for the supply or acquisition of those goods or services will not exceed AUD 3 million in any twelve-month period (or higher amounts as set by regulation): section 93AB(4).

113. The reasonable expectation must exist at the time of the giving of the collective bargaining notice, and if the initial contract has been made, at the time it was made: section 93AB(5). A collective bargaining notice may be given on behalf of one or more of the contracting parties, providing each could have given notice on

79. As set out in the *Competition and Consumer Act Regulations 2010.*

their own behalf: section 93AB(7). A corporation may not give a collective bargaining notice in relation to a contract or proposed contract where an application for authorization has been made to the ACCC in relation to that contract or proposed contract, which has been dismissed, and either no application for review of that decision has been made to the Tribunal, or if made, the Tribunal has determined that application: section 93AB(8). Provided the collective bargaining notification is valid, immunity from legal action for the notified collective bargaining arrangement begins at the conclusion of a statutory period. Until 31 December 2008, the statutory period was twenty-eight days from the date a valid notification is lodged. From 1 January 2009, the statutory period is fourteen days from the date a valid notification is lodged: section 93AD. Once a collective bargaining notice comes into force, it remains in force for a period of three years, unless it is earlier withdrawn, or if the Commission gives an objection notice, on the date specified by the ACCC in the objection notice: section 93AD(3). If the ACCC issues a draft objection notice within the fourteen-(or twenty-eight) day period, immunity does not commence. If a draft objection notice is issued after the fourteen-(or twenty-eight) day period, protection from legal action does commence and continues until the revocation is complete. If the ACCC subsequently issues a final objection notice, any immunity that was provided by the notification is removed thirty-one days after the date of the objection notice or on a later day specified by the ACCC: section 93AD(3)(b). Decisions made by the ACCC to revoke immunity can be reviewed by the ACT. Any immunity that might have been in place continues until the appeal process concludes. The ACCC will issue an objection notice, if it is satisfied that any public benefit that has resulted or is likely to result, or would result or be likely to result, from the provision does not or would not outweigh the detriment to the public that has resulted or is likely to result, or would result or be likely to result, from the provision: section 93AC(1).

114. If the collective bargaining notice relates to a provision of the kind referred to in section 45(1)(a) or (b), then the ACCC may, if it is satisfied that:

a. the provision has or would have the purpose, or has or is likely to have, or would have or be likely to have, the effect of substantially lessening competition, and
b. in all the circumstances, either:
   - the provision has not resulted or is not likely to result, or would not result or be likely to result, in a benefit to the public, or
   - any benefit to the public that has resulted or is likely to result, or would result or be likely to result, from the provision, does not or would not outweigh the detriment to the public constituted by any lessening of competition that has resulted or is likely to result, or would result or be likely to result, from the provision, give the corporation an objection notice stating that it is so satisfied: section 93AC(2).

The ACCC must give the corporation, at the time it gives an objection notice, a written statement of its reasons for giving the notice: section 93AC(3).

D. Other Institutional Tasks (Consultancy to Parliament/Government)

115. The ACCC can make recommendations to the Federal Parliament and the government in relation to proposed amendments to competition and consumer law and policy (section 28(1) CCA). The ACCC also has six consultative committees and two forums with external stakeholders:

- ACCC Performance Consultative Committee.
- Consumer Consultative Committee.
- Franchising Consultative Committee.
- Fuel Consultative Committee.
- Infrastructure Consultative Committee.
- Small Business Consultative Committee.
- Utility Regulators Forum.
- Wholesaler Telecommunications Consultative Committee.

116. Each of these committees is a forum for policy development and industry discussions. These groups also provide accountability and transparency to the ACCC's decision and policymaking.

II. Government Direct Enforcement Activities

117. Public enforcement is via the regulator, the ACCC.

III. Other Administrative Agencies Applying Antitrust Rules

118. The ACCC is the independent statutory government authority that administers the CCA.

IV. Administrative Fines

119. The ACCC does not have the power to issue an administrative fine, although it can seek court-enforceable undertakings (pursuant to section 87B of the CCA) from entities. Should the ACCC wish to seek a fine, it must do so through the court system, and these are known as pecuniary penalties. However, strictly speaking they are not a fine as such, the proceedings are civil in nature, and the civil standard of proof will apply – that is the balance of probabilities (section 77 CCA).

120. A civil penalty of up to AUD 500,000 can be imposed on an individual.

121. Section 76(1) gives the court general guidelines on the level of pecuniary penalty to be imposed for Part IV contraventions. It has been described as a process of instinctive synthesis.[80]

V. Administrative Injunctions and Other Restrictive Orders

122. In the competition field, the ACCC does not have the power to unilaterally impose administrative injunctions and other restrictive orders. It must seek a court decision to that effect.

VI. Interim Measures

123. Under section 80(2) of the CCA, the Federal Court of Australia (FCA) has the power to grant an interim injunction where, in the court's opinion, it is desirable to do so.

§2. Civil Enforcement

124. Civil enforcement occurs by way of public enforcement by Australia's competition regulator, the ACCC and private enforcement by those who have suffered or are likely to suffer loss as a result of conduct that contravenes competition laws.

I. Competent Civil Courts

125. Jurisdiction to determine civil liability under the CCA is conferred on the FCA.[81] Appeals from trial decisions are heard by the Full Court of the FCA. Appeals from Full Court decisions are heard by Australia's highest appellate court, the High Court of Australia.

II. Sanctions

A. *Nullity*

1. Contracts

126. At common law, a presumption of illegality and unenforceability arises where the making of a contract involves an illegal act. However, section 4L of the

80. *Australian Competition and Consumer Commission v Cement Australia Pty Ltd and Others* (2016) 242 FCR 389.
81. Section 86(1) *Competition and Consumer Act 2010.*

CCA provides for a different outcome where contracts contravene competition laws because of the inclusion of a particular provision in the contract. Section 4L provides that if the making of a contract contravenes competition laws because the contract includes a particular provision then that provision should be severed, and the remainder of the contract remains valid and enforceable.[82] The common law severance rules do not apply as section 4L has been interpreted as requiring, rather than permitting the severance of offending conditions.[83]

127. Even though section 4L operates to preserve the validity of contracts of the kind outlined in the preceding paragraph, such contracts may be declared void (in whole or in part) or varied if a party to the proceeding seeks such an order under section 87 of the CCA.[84] Section 87 gives the court the discretion to make such an order where a party to the proceeding has suffered or is likely to suffer loss or damage as a result of a contravention of competition laws, provided that making such an order will prevent or reduce the loss or damage.[85]

2. Divestiture

128. A court has the power to order, by way of mandatory injunction, divestiture of shares or assets acquired in contravention of the merger prohibition.[86] Divestiture may also be ordered where a merger clearance or authorization was granted on the basis of false or misleading information.[87] A court may declare a merger that breaches the merger prohibition void if the vendor was involved in the contravention, and the assets and shares acquired in contravention of the prohibition are still vested in the acquirer.[88] A divestiture need not be total. As the provision that gives the court the power to order divestiture is not penal, the court is only likely to order divestiture to the extent necessary to ensure that the merger in question no longer substantially lessens competition.[89] Divestiture actions must be brought within three years of the merger[90] and, unlike injunctions to restrain a merger, can be brought by any person.

129. A court may also accept undertakings by the acquirer to dispose of shares or assets in lieu of making a divestiture order.[91]

---

82. Section 4L *Competition and Consumer Act 2010.*
83. *SST Consulting Services Pty Limited v. Rieson* (2006) 225 CLR 516, 533.
84. See, for example, *ASX Operations Pty Ltd v. Pont Data Australia Pty Ltd* (1991) 27 FCR 460.
85. Section 87 *Competition and Consumer Act 2010.*
86. Section 80(1) *Competition and Consumer Act 2010.*
87. Section 81A *Competition and Consumer Act 2010.*
88. Section 80(1A) *Competition and Consumer Act 2010.*
89. *Trade Practices Commission v. Australia Meat Holdings Pty Ltd* (1988) 83 ALR 299.
90. Section 80(2) *Competition and Consumer Act 2010.*
91. Section 80(1C) *Competition and Consumer Act 2010.*

B. Damages

130. Section 82 of the CCA provides that a person who suffers loss or damage by conduct of another that was done in contravention of a competition law provision may recover the amount of the loss or damage by action against that other person or any person involved in the contravention.[92] A person will be held to be involved in a corporation where that person:[93]

- aided, abetted, counselled or procured the contravention;
- induced the contravention;
- was knowingly concerned in the contravention; or
- conspired with others to effect the contravention.

131. An action for damages must be commenced within six years of the cause of action that relates to the conduct accruing.[94] As damages can only be awarded under section 82, where loss or damage has been suffered, the cause of action accrues at this point in time, not when the contravening conduct occurred.[95]

132. Findings of fact made against a respondent in an earlier proceeding may be relied upon by a plaintiff as prima facie evidence of those facts in later proceedings for damages.[96] Despite this, private actions in relation to breaches of competition law provisions are relatively rare in Australia,[97] although there is some evidence that this trend is reversing.[98]

133. Section 87 gives the court the power to order the contravener to pay compensation for loss or damage likely to be suffered as a result of the contravention.[99] Where a section 87 order is sought on its own, the claim must be brought within six years of the cause of action that relates to the conduct accruing.[100] The claim must be brought within the same period of time where a section 87 order is sought in conjunction with a claim for damages under section 82. Where a section 87 order is sought in conjunction with proceedings seeking the imposition of pecuniary penalties, the claim must be brought within three years. As the cause of action accrues when the applicant suffers or is likely to suffer loss, time will generally start to run when the contravening conduct occurs as this is the point in time when the likelihood of loss arises.

---

92. Section 82(1) *Competition and Consumer Act 2010.*
93. Section 75B *Competition and Consumer Act 2010.*
94. Section 82(2) *Competition and Consumer Act 2010.*
95. *Wardley Australia Ltd v. State of Western Australia* (1992) 175 CLR 514. See also *Arcadi v. Colonial Mutual Life Assurance Society Ltd* (1984) ATPR para. 40-473.
96. Section 83 *Competition and Consumer Act 2010.*
97. Maureen Brunt, 'The Role of Private Actions in Australian Restrictive Practices Enforcement', *Melbourne University Law Review* 17 (1990): 582.
98. A class action was brought by consumers who were overcharged as a result of the international vitamins cartel (*Bray v. Hoffman-La Roche Ltd* (2002) 118 FCR 1). This action was ultimately settled.
99. Sections 87(1), 87(2)(d) *Competition and Consumer Act 2010.*
100. Section 87(1CA) *Competition and Consumer Act 2010.*

1. Civil Penalties

134. The ACCC may bring proceedings seeking the imposition of civil pecuniary penalties upon those who contravene or attempt to contravene the competition law prohibition in the CCA.[101] An attempt will be made out where a person has taken a step towards the commission of a contravention.[102] It is not necessary to show that the attempt has reached an advanced stage. An action in which the imposition of pecuniary penalties is sought must be brought within six years of the contravention.[103]

135. Pecuniary penalties can also be sought against an individual or company who:

- aids, abets, counsels or procures the contravention of;
- induces, or attempts to induce, the contravention of;
- is in any way knowingly concerned in, or party to, the contravention of; or
- conspires with others to contravene;
- the competition law prohibitions.

All of the circumstances listed above require that the individual or company involved in the contravention was a knowing participant.[104]

136. Pecuniary penalties are not fines, so the civil standard of proof applies.[105] Thus the ACCC must be able to establish the contravention to the civil standard, namely on the balance of probabilities. However, this standard is flexible; the graver the allegation, the greater the strictness of proof required.[106] Nevertheless, the required standard of proof is clearly lower than that which would apply at a criminal trial.

137. The maximum civil penalty a court can impose on a body corporate that contravenes the prohibition against anticompetitive agreements, cartel agreements, misuse of market power, exclusive dealing, resale price maintenance or mergers that substantially lessen competition is the greater of the following:

---

101. Sections 76, 77(1) *Competition and Consumer Act 2010.*
102. *Trade Practices Commission v. Parkfield Operations Pty Ltd* (1985) 7 FCR 534.
103. Section 77(2) *Competition and Consumer Act 2010.*
104. *Yorke v. Lucas* (1985) 158 CLR 661, 667.
105. Section 78 *Competition and Consumer Act 2010*; *The Heating Centre Pty Ltd v. Trade Practices Commission* (1986) 9 FCR 153. See also *Setka and Another v Magistrates Court of Victoria and Another* (2017) 323 FCR 108 where s, 78 could not be used as a defence to a charge of blackmail. It was argued that as s, 78 offers immunity in respect of criminal proceedings then the charge could not be sustained. This was dismissed as the immunity offered by s, 78 was only in respect of conduct that would amount to no more than a contravention of the competition legislation. As the conduct went beyond what would result in a contravention of the competition legislation, the immunity could not apply.
106. *Briginshaw v. Briginshaw* (1938) 60 CLR 336; *Trade Practices Commission v. Ansett Transport Industries (Operations) Pty Ltd* (1978) 32 FLR 305, 329.

- AUD 10,000,000;
- three times the value of the benefit obtained as a result of the contravention (where this can be determined); or
- (where the court cannot determine the value of the benefit obtained), 10% of the annual turnover of the body corporate during the period of twelve months ending at the end of the month in which the contravention occurred.

138. The maximum penalty the court can impose on a body corporate that contravenes the specific prohibitions against secondary boycotts,[107] boycotts directed against the movement of goods to and from Australia,[108] and indirect secondary boycotts[109] is AUD 750,000.

139. The maximum penalty that can be imposed against an individual involved in a contravention is AUD 500,000.[110] In addition, the court may also make an order disqualifying a person from managing corporations for a particular period.[111] Corporations cannot indemnify officers, employees or agents against the imposition of a pecuniary penalty upon such persons.[112] Any attempt to do so could result in the imposition of an AUD 2,750 penalty upon the indemnifying entity.[113]

140. In *Trade Practices Commission v. CSR Ltd*,[114] it was indicated that the primary aim of penalties is to deter repetition by the contravener (specific deterrence) and by others who may be tempted to engage in similar conduct (general deterrence). His Honour stated that the following factors should be taken into account when penalties are being determined:

- the nature and extent of the contravening conduct;
- the amount of loss or damage caused;
- the circumstances in which the conduct took place;
- the size of the contravening company;
- the degree of power it has, as evidenced by its market share and ease of entry into the market;
- the deliberateness of the contravention and the period over which it extended;[115]
- whether the contravention arose out of senior management or at a lower level;[116]
- whether the company has a corporate culture conducive to compliance (as evidenced, for example, by an effective compliance programme); and

107. Sections 45D, 45EA *Competition and Consumer Act 2010.*
108. Sections 45DB, 45EA *Competition and Consumer Act 2010.*
109. Sections 45E, 45EA *Competition and Consumer Act 2010.*
110. Section 76(1B) *Competition and Consumer Act 2010.*
111. Section 86E *Competition and Consumer Act 2010.*
112. Section 77A *Competition and Consumer Act 2010.*
113. Section 77B *Competition and Consumer Act 2010.*
114. *Trade Practices Commission v. CSR Ltd* (1991) paras 52-135, 52-152.
115. See also *Australian Competition and Consumer Commission v. Leahy Petroleum (No. 2)* (2005) 215 ALR 218, 286.
116. See also *Australian Competition and Consumer Commission v. Leahy Petroleum (No. 2)* (2005) 215 ALR 218, 293.

– whether the company has shown a disposition to cooperate with the ACCC.[117]

141. Whether the contravening corporation has previously engaged in similar conduct in the past and the contravener's financial position will be taken into account.[118] Whether the respondent instigated the conduct is also a relevant consideration.[119] The fact that a company acted on the basis of inaccurate legal advice provides no excuse,[120] although such advice may be relevant to the consideration of the deliberateness of the conduct.[121] However, where the conduct is plainly and deliberately motivated by a desire to reduce competition, the fact that a company has been advised that it will not contravene the competition laws is of little relevance.[122]

142. The ACCC may negotiate a penalty with the contravener, especially where the contravener has cooperated with the ACCC during its investigations. The court is not bound by the agreement or proposal reached although it will consider any submission made by the ACCC relating to penalties when reaching its decision.[123] The courts have also demonstrated an awareness of the fact that negotiated settlements free ACCC resources that can be used to detect other forms of anticompetitive conduct.[124] In *ACCC v. NW Frozen Foods Pty Ltd*,[125] the parties had agreed on a penalty of AUD 900,000. The judge considered that this was too low and substituted a penalty of AUD 1.2 million. On appeal, the agreed settlement was reinstated – the Full Court of the Federal Court[126] considering that a court should not depart from the agreed figure simply because it was disposed to adopt another figure.

143. Where a civil penalty has been imposed, the court also has the power to order the contravener to publish an advertisement, at its expense, disclosing that it breached competition laws and explaining the nature of that breach.[127]

---

117. See also *Australian Competition and Consumer Commission v. NW Frozen Foods Pty Ltd* (1996) 71 FCR 285, 293–294.
118. *Australian Competition and Consumer Commission v. NW Frozen Foods Pty Ltd* (1996) para. 42-435.
119. *Australian Competition and Consumer Commission v. Leahy Petroleum (No. 2)* (2005) 215 ALR 218.
120. *Universal Music Australia Pty Ltd v. Australian Competition and Consumer Commission* (2003) 131 FCR 529.
121. *Australian Competition and Consumer Commission v. Anglo Estates Pty Ltd* (2005) ATPR para. 42-044, [53].
122. *Universal Music Australia Pty Ltd v. Australian Competition and Consumer Commission* (2003) 131 FCR 529, 598–599.
123. *Australian Competition and Consumer Commission v. SIP Australia Pty Ltd* (1999) ATPR paras 41-702, 43,000.
124. *Trade Practices Commission v. TNT Australia Pty Limited* (1995) ATPR paras 41-375, 40-164 – 40-165.
125. [1996] ATPR para. 41-515.
126. *NW Frozen Foods Pty Ltd v. ACCC* (1996) 71 FCR 285.
127. Section 86D *Competition and Consumer Act 2010*.

C. Interim Measures

1. Injunction

144. The court has the power to grant final (permanent)[128] and interlocutory (interim)[129] injunctions to restrain breaches or attempted breaches of competition laws. The court may grant a mandatory injunction (which requires the party to whom it is addressed to do something) or a prohibitory injunction (which requires the party to whom it is addressed to refrain from doing something). Most injunctions sought in the competition law context are prohibitory in nature. However, the courts have been willing to grant mandatory injunctions ordering a party who has breached competition laws to supply a product at a particular price where the open market or prior dealings between the parties provide a reference point against which a pricing order can be framed.[130] The court also has the power to accept an undertaking in lieu of granting an injunction.[131]

145. With the exception of merger activity, any person may apply to the court for an injunction to restrain conduct that would breach the competition law prohibitions. Only the ACCC may apply for an injunction to restrain a proposed acquisition from taking place.[132] Courts have the power to grant an injunction restraining a person from engaging in particular forms of conduct whether or not it appears that the person intends to engage again or continue to engage in the conduct and whether or not the person has previously engaged in conduct of that kind.[133] An injunction can also be granted irrespective of whether there is an imminent danger of substantial damage to any person if the potential contravener engaged in conduct sought to be restrained by the injunction.[134]

146. An interlocutory injunction is an injunction designed to last until trial or further order or to last until a specified date or further order. As it can take quite a while to bring a case before the courts, interim injunctions provide an important mechanism from protecting against harm that could be caused by anticompetitive conduct before the matter comes before the courts. Interim injunctions are usually only granted in *inter partes* proceedings so that the defendant has an opportunity to present its case.

147. Courts adopt a two-stage test when determining whether to grant an interlocutory injunction. A plaintiff will be granted an injunction if the following two requirements are met. First, the plaintiff must establish that there is a serious question to be tried. This requirement will generally be satisfied where the claim is not

128. Section 80(1) *Competition and Consumer Act 2010.*
129. Section 80(2) *Competition and Consumer Act 2010.*
130. *Maclean v. Shell Chemical (Australia) Pty Ltd* (1984) 2 FCR 593; *O'Keeffe Nominees Pty Ltd v. BP Australia Ltd* (1990) ATPR para. 41-057.
131. *Thomson Australia Holdings Pty Ltd v. Trade Practices* (1981) 148 CLR 150.
132. Section 80(1A) *Competition and Consumer Act 2010.*
133. Section 80(4)(a)–(b) *Competition and Consumer Act 2010.*
134. Section 80(4)(c) *Competition and Consumer Act 2010.*

frivolous or vexatious. Second, the plaintiff must establish that the balance of convenience favours the applicant.[135] The applicant's need for protection is weighed against the need for the defendant to be protected against injury resulting from it having been restrained from engaging in the conduct in question. If the applicant's needs outweigh the defendant's, the second requirement will be satisfied. Where the applicant would be adequately compensated by an award of damages, it is unlikely that the balance of convenience will favour the applicant. However, if the conduct is likely to cause irreparable harm to the applicant's business, or in a case brought by the ACCC where the conduct is likely to impose significant costs on society, the second requirement is more likely to be satisfied. In the context of mergers, the courts have taken the view that the availability of the remedy of divestiture significantly reduces the need to grant an interlocutory injunction because in the event that the merger goes ahead and is found to breach the merger prohibition, it can effectively be reversed.[136] The balance of convenience is likely to favour the respondent because if an interlocutory injunction is granted, irreparable harm to the respondent is almost inevitable if the merger does not in fact breach the merger prohibition.

D. Other Orders

1. Compliance Programmes

148. The courts often order a party that has breached competition laws to implement a compliance programme.[137] It is common for such orders to require the contravener to have its compliance programme audited.

2. Undertakings

149. As an alternative to litigation, the ACCC may accept court-enforceable undertakings designed to prevent a recurrence of the offending conduct.[138] If such undertakings are breached, the court may issue an order directing the person who gave the undertaking to:

- comply with its terms;
- pay the Commonwealth an amount up to the amount of any financial benefit that the person has obtained that is attributable to the breach; and/or
- compensate any person who has suffered loss or damage as a result of the breach.

135. *Epitoma Pty Ltd v. Australasian Meat Industry Employees' Union* (1984) 3 FCR 55, 58.
136. *APM Investments Pty Ltd v. Trade Practices Commission* (1983) 49 ALR 475, 485.
137. Section 86C of the *Competition and Consumer Act 2010* gives the court the power to make such orders.
138. Section 87B *Competition and Consumer Act 2010*; see also ACCC, *Section 87B of the Competition and Consumer Act* (September 2009).

150. Parties may offer structural or behavioural undertakings. Structural undertakings are directed at structural issues in the relevant markets. Behavioural undertakings are directed at the way the merged entity will behave in the future on an ongoing basis. The ACCC has a strong preference for structural undertakings as behavioural undertakings can be difficult to monitor and enforce and may also be inflexible and unresponsive to market changes.

E. Other Orders

151. Section 87 also provides that the court may make such orders 'as it thinks fit' in proceedings for breach of the CCA. These orders may be made where a party to the proceedings has suffered or is likely to suffer loss or damage as a result of the conduct of persons engaging in the conduct or involved in the contravention if the court considers that the order will compensate such damage in whole or in part. The intent of section 87 is to enable the court to make orders other than an injunction (a declaration or damages) where such other order may more effectively compensate an applicant for loss or damage that it has suffered or may suffer because of contravening conduct. Section 87(2), (3) and (4) specify the types of orders that may be made by a court under section 87. These are the orders:

- declaring the whole or any part of a contract to be void and, if the court thinks fit, to have been void *ab initio* (section 87(2)(a));
- varying a contract or arrangement (section 87(2)(b));
- refusing to enforce any or all of the provisions of a contract (section 87(2)(ba));
- directing a refund of money or the return of property to the person who has suffered the loss or damage (section 87(2)(c));
- directing the person who engaged in the conduct or who was involved in the contravention to pay the amount of the loss or damage (section 87(2)(d));
- order directing the person who engaged in the conduct or who was involved in the contravention, at his or her own expense, to repair or provide parts for goods supplied (section 87(2)(e));
- directing the person who engaged in the conduct or who was involved in the contravention, at his or her own expense, to supply specified services (section 87(2)(f));
- in relation to an instrument creating or transferring an interest in land, the person who engaged in the conduct or who was involved in the contravention, to execute an instrument that varies or terminates the instrument (section 87(2)(g));
- varying a covenant or collateral arrangement (section 87(3)(c));
- directing another party to the contract or entitled to the benefit of the covenant to do any acts that the court considers just and equitable (section 87(3)(d)); and
- directing the termination of a lease or the increase or reduction of any rent or premium payable under a lease (section 87(4)).

152. Section 87B authorizes the ACCC to accept an undertaking in relation to any matter in which the ACCC has a power or function under the CCA. Such undertakings are in the nature of consent injunctions and avoid the need for a trial. In the event of a breach, the court may make all or any of the orders set out in section 87(4):

- an order directing the person to comply with the terms of the undertaking (section 87B(4)(a));
- an order directing the person pay the Commonwealth of Australia an amount up to the amount of any financial benefit that the person has obtained directly or indirectly and that is reasonably attributable to the breach (section 87B(4)(b));
- an order the court considers appropriate directing the person to pay compensation to any other person who has suffered loss or damage as a result of the breach (section 87B(4)(c)); and
- any other order that the court thinks appropriate (section 87B(4)(d)).

153. By virtue of section 163A, the FCA has powers to make orders (in the nature of prohibition, certiorari or mandamus) and declarations in relation to the operation or effect of any provision of the CCA or in relation to the validity of any act or thing done, proposed or purported to be done under the CCA. The jurisdiction is to hear and determine any proceeding or cross-proceeding in which a party is seeking such relief. This is a specific head of jurisdiction relating to 'matters' arising under the CCA and is additional to the general jurisdiction of the court conferred by section 21 of the *Federal Court of Australia Act 1976*.

F. Cost Orders

154. The judge has an absolute and unfettered discretion to award costs in competition law matters.[139] Absent special circumstances, the successful litigant will usually receive its costs. However, where the successful party has succeeded only upon a portion of his claim, it may be reasonable that it bear the expense of litigating the portion that failed. In such circumstances, the successful party may also be ordered to pay the costs of the unsuccessful party that relate to the portion that failed.[140]

---

139. Section 43 *Federal Court of Australia Act* 1976; *Trade Practices Commission v. Nicholas Enterprises Pty Ltd (No. 1)* (1978) 26 ALR 126.
140. *Ritter v. Godfrey* (1920) 2 KB 47; *Forster v. Farquhar* (1893) 1 QB 564; *Cretazzo v. Lombardi* (1975) 13 SASR 4. These principles were accepted in the competition law context in *Hughes v. Western Australian Cricket Association* (1986) paras 40-748, 48-136 and *Australian Competition and Consumer Commission v. Australian Safeway Stores Pty Ltd (No. 3)*[2003] FCAFC 163.

§3. Criminal Enforcement

I. Criminal Sanctions for Antitrust Violations

155. Part IV, Division 1 establishes cartel offence for:

- price-fixing;
- market sharing;
- bid-rigging; and
- arrangements that restrict output.

156. The ACCC has enhanced investigatory powers to assist with criminal sanctions:

- The ACCC can use telephone interception warrants (such as, 'phone taps' and surveillance device warrants) upon application by an interception agency or law enforcement officer other than the ACCC (such as the Australian Federal Police) for criminal cartel investigations. The ACCC will need to determine that it is investigating a criminal matter, not a civil prohibition, and liaise accordingly with bodies such as the Australian Federal Police.
- The definition of 'executing officer' has been expanded so that the ACCC inspector originally named in a warrant to enter premises under Part XID of the CCA does not have to be present to execute the warrant.
- The executing officers and officers assisting are permitted to 'take a break' in the execution of a warrant under Part XID of the CCA and leave the premises for up to an hour (or longer period if the occupier of the premises consents in writing).
- The ACCC will be allowed, in certain circumstances under Part XID of the CCA, to remove a 'thing' from the premises being searched for up to seventy-two hours (subject to extension) for examination or processing in order to determine whether it may be seized under the warrant.
- A member of the Australian Federal Police, as an officer assisting in the execution of a warrant under Part XID of the CCA, may use 'such force against persons and things as is necessary and reasonable in the circumstances'.
- The executing officer under Part XID of the CCA is permitted to apply to a magistrate for an order requiring a 'specified person' to provide any information or assistance, that is reasonable and necessary, to allow the officer to access data held in (or accessible from) a computer on the premises, transfer the data to a disk or other storage device or convert the data into documentary form. The 'specified person' may be a person reasonably suspected of having committed the contravention, the owner or lessee of the computer or an employee of the owner or lessee. A person who breaches the order is liable to imprisonment for six months.

157. Criminal sanctions can only be imposed on those who breach the cartel offence provisions. All other competition law violations are only punishable by the imposition of civil pecuniary penalties.

158. A corporation that breaches or attempts to breach a cartel provision offence is punishable by a fine not exceeding the greater of the following:[141]

- AUD 10,000,000;
- three times the total of the value of the benefit obtained by one or more persons and the benefits reasonably attributable to the commission of the offence (where this can be determined); or
- (where the court cannot determine the total of the value of the benefits obtained), 10% of the corporation's annual turnover during the period of twelve months ending at the end of the month in which the corporation committed, or began committing the offence.[142]

159. Civil cartel offences are proven on the balance of probabilities. Should criminal sanctions such as gaol be sought against an individual, the elements of the offence must be proved beyond reasonable doubt. The operation of this legislation can be seen in *Australian Competition & Consumer Commission v. Renegade Gas Pty Ltd (trading as Supagas NSW).*[143] This saw pecuniary penalties of AUD 4.8 million imposed on the lead corporate party involved in the cartel, with the lesser party being ordered to AUD 3.1 million (the cartel being one to stay away from customers of a competitor). The natural persons that orchestrated the cartel paid pecuniary penalties ranging from AUD 50,000 to AUD 250,000.

160. An individual who:

- attempts to contravene;
- aids, abets, counsels or procures the contravention of;
- induces, or attempts to induce, the contravention of;
- is in any way knowingly concerned in, or party to, the contravention of;
- conspires with others to contravene the cartel provision offence is punishable by;
- a term of imprisonment not exceeding ten years;
- a fine not exceeding AUD 220,000; or
- both.

141. Sections 44ZZRF(3), 44ZZRG(3) *Competition and Consumer Act 2010.*
142. An example of the provision of penalties for a breach of s. 45 can be seen in *Australian Competition and Consumer Commission v. Emirates* [2012] FCA 1108 where Emirates was required to pay penalties totalling AUD 10ml., for giving effect to undertakings in relation to fuel surcharge, security and customs fees. See also *Australian Competition and Consumer Commission v. Malaysia Airline System Berhad (No. 2)* [2012] FCA 767; *Australian Competition and Consumer Commission v. April International Marketing Services Australia Pt Ltd (No. 8)* (2011) 277 ALR 446. The first prosecution under the cartel provisions saw a penalty of (AUD) $25ml imposed. The court reflected that the cartel conduct warrants denunciation and that this sort of behaviour was inimical and destructive of the free-market economy of Australia, and consequently damaging to business and consumers. But for the willingness of the accused to cooperate, the penalty would have been significantly higher: *Director of Public Prosecutions (Cth) v Nippon Yusen Kabushkik Kaisha* (2017) 254 FCR 235.
143. [2014] FCA 1135. See also *Norcat S AR L v. Bradken Ltd (No. 2)* [2013] 219 FCR 14; [2013] FCA 235.

161. Criminal prosecution in relation to cartel conduct will commence with committal proceedings before a magistrate in a state or territory court. If the magistrate decides that the charges are sufficiently strong, the accused will be committed to stand trial.

II. Other Application of Criminal Law to Relevant Conducts

162. In Australia, antitrust matters will be solely examined under the provisions of the CCA.

III. Role of Prosecutor

163. The ACCC is responsible for investigating cartel conduct. The Commonwealth Director of Public Prosecutions (CDPP) is responsible for prosecuting breaches of the cartel provision offences upon referral from the ACCC.[144]

164. When deciding whether cartel conduct is sufficiently serious to warrant referral to the CDPP the ACCC will consider whether:

- the conduct was longstanding;
- the conduct has a significant impact on the market;
- one or more of the alleged participants had engaged in cartel conduct before; and
- the value of affected commerce exceeded AUD 1 million within a twelve-month period.

165. Upon referral, the CDPP will advise the ACCC whether a criminal prosecution should be commenced. The CDPP will consider whether there is sufficient evidence to prosecute the case and whether the public interest requires a prosecution.

IV. Competent Criminal Courts

166. Jurisdiction to determine criminal liability under the CCA is conferred on the FCA.[145] The matter will be decided by a jury. Appeals from trial decisions are heard by the Full Court of the FCA. Appeals from Full Court decisions are heard by Australia's highest appellate court, the High Court of Australia.

144. See further Memoranda of Understanding, *Australian Competition and Consumer Commission re Serious Cartel Conduct* (2014).

145. Section 4 *Competition and Consumer Act 2010* provides that a reference to the court means the Federal Court of Australia. The *Federal Court of Australia Amendment (Criminal Jurisdiction) Act* 2009 conferred indictable criminal jurisdiction on the Federal Court.

Part II. The Application of the Prohibitions

Chapter 1. Restrictive Agreements

§1. Horizontal Agreements

I. Cartels

167. Section 45AA and section 45 of the CCA prohibits agreements that have the purpose or effect or likely effect of substantially lessening competition, or which contain a cartel provision. Engaging in concerted practices will also breach the provision. Breaching these provisions can involve ACCC seeking remedial relief.

168. Individuals may apply to the court for:

- injunctions;
- damages; and
- ancillary orders.

169. A cartel offence (*see* Part IV, Division 1) is also punishable by imprisonment of up to ten years and/or a fine of 2,000 penalty units per contravention. Authorization immunity is available for section 45 practices under section 88 of the CCA. The key ingredient in section 45 is collusion. Without actual or attempted collusion, there can be no contravention of this section. Provided the parties are engaging in independent decision-making, no breach is likely to be established. To establish a cartel offence, it must be shown that the parties' cartel provision had the requisite purpose or effect **and** that the parties were in competition with each other (section 45AD).

170. Section 45(1) states:

(1) A corporation must not:
  (a) make a contract or arrangement, or arrive at an understanding, if a provision of the proposed contract, arrangement or understanding has the purpose, or would have or be likely to have the effect, of substantially lessening competition;
  (b) give effect to a provision of a contract, arrangement or understanding, if that provision has the purpose, or has or is likely to have the effect, of substantially lessening competition; or

(c) engage with one or more persons in a concerted practice that has the purpose, or has or is likely to have the effect, of substantially lessening competition.

171. As noted, the critical ingredient to breach section 45 is collusion, which in the Australian legislation requires a contract, arrangement or understanding. Obviously, arrangement or understanding has a broader focus than contract, and it is these terms that have come under scrutiny. For example in *Newton v. Federal Commissioner of Taxation,*[146] it was stated that: 'the word arrangement is apt to describe something less than a binding contract or agreement, something in the nature of an understanding between two or more persons – a plan arranged between them which may not be enforceable at law'. Similarly, in the oft-quoted *Re British Basic Slag*[147] Wilmer LJ noted:

> Although it may not be easy to put into words, everyone knows what it is meant by arrangement between two or more parties. If the arrangement is intended to be enforceable by legal proceedings as in the case where it is made for good consideration, it may no doubt properly be described as an agreement. But the statute clearly contemplates that there may be arrangements which are not enforceable by legal proceedings, but which create only moral or obligations binding in honour .... For, when each of two or more parties intentionally arouse in the others an expectation that he will act in a certain way, it seems to me that he incurs at least a moral obligation to do so. An arrangement as so defined is thereby something 'whereby the parties to it accept mutual rights and obligations'.

172. In Top Performance Motors Pty Ltd v. Ira Berk (Qld) Pty Ltd[148] Smithers J. stated:

> It seems to me also that an understanding must involve the meeting of two or more minds. Where the minds of the parties are at one that a proposed transaction between them proceeds on the basis of the maintenance of a particular state of affairs or the adoption of a particular course of conduct, it would seem that there would be an understanding within the meaning of the Act.

173. A factual expectation alone will not meet the requisite standard of an understanding.[149] Where there is no commitment between the parties, no reciprocity of obligation and only unilateral action, there will be no collusion as required by the legislation.[150] It is possible to infer collusion from circumstantial evidence.

146. (1958) 98 CLR 1 at 7.
147. [1963] 2 All ER 807, 819.
148. (1975) 24 FLR 286 at 291, 5 ALR 465, ATPR 40-004 at 17-116.
149. *Apco Service Stations v. ACCC* [2005] ATPR 42-078, [46].
150. *Apco Service Stations v. ACCC* [2005] ATPR 42-078.

174. Where conduct may well breach both section 45 (dealing with horizontal arrangements) and section 47 (dealing with vertical arrangements), section 45(5A) & 45(6) provides as follows:

(5A) The making of a contract, arrangement or understanding does not constitute a contravention of this section because the contract, arrangement or understanding contains a provision the giving effect to which would, or would apart from subsection 47(10) or section 88 or 93, constitute a contravention of section 47.

(6) This section does not apply to or in relation to the giving effect to a provision of a contract, arrangement or understanding, or to or in relation to engaging in a concerted practice, by way of:

(a) engaging in conduct that contravenes, or would but for the operation of subsection 47(10) or section 88 or 93 contravene, section 47; or

(b) doing an act by reason of a breach or threatened breach of a condition referred to in subsection 47(2), (4), (6) or (8), being an act done by a person at a time when:

(i) an authorization under section 88 is in force in relation to conduct engaged in by that person on that condition; or

(ii) by reason of subsection 93(7) conduct engaged in by that person on that condition is not to be taken to have the effect of substantially lessening competition within the meaning of section 47; or

(iii) a notice under subsection 93(1) is in force in relation to conduct engaged in by that person on that condition.

175. The High Court of Australia in *Visy Paper v. ACCC*[151] considered the interpretation of this provision. Visy and another entity were competitors in the waste paper industry. Visy also agreed to acquire waste paper from this other entity on the basis that it would not collect waste paper from customers of Visy. If this was exclusive dealing, it would fall for consideration under section 47 and be excluded via the terms of 45(6) as they stood then from consideration of section 45. If the restraint was considered as a supply of services, it was caught by section 47(4); if it was the acquisition of goods, it was not. Whereas the primary judge considered that as section 47 could potentially be invoked, the matter was thereby removed from section 45, the High Court disagreed. Only if the clause were wholly within the province of section 47 would it be removed from section 45. The importance of this decision was that under section 47, the test was one of substantially lessening competition. Under section 45, it was a per se breach (as the legislation stood at the time). Having found that section 45 could apply, Visy was found liable.

176. Section 45 will also not be breached where the corporation proposes to enter a collective bargaining arrangement between a group (e.g., farmers) and a target (such as a processing company) (section 93AB). This is permitted where the

151. (2003) 216 CLR 1.

value of the arrangement between the group and the target is unlikely to exceed AUD 3 million in a twelve-month window. The Commission may object to a collective bargaining notice.

177. Once a contract, arrangement or understanding is established, the next question is whether the contract, arrangement or understanding substantially lessened competition. The latter provision requires proof of the market, and consideration of whether the purpose or effect of the contract, arrangement or understanding was to lead to a substantial lessening of competition. An illustration of this can be seen in *Rural Press v. ACCC.*[152] Rural Press published a newspaper, the *Murray Valley Standard.* This was circulated in the Murray Bridge district of South Australia. Further along the Murray River in the Riverland region, Waikerie Printing published the *River News.* For the most part, the two newspapers did not compete. Following a council restructure, Waikerie started to distribute the *River News* in the Murray Bridge area. The paper was now in direct competition with the *Murray Valley Standard.* Rural Press threatened Waikerie that if it did not withdraw, it would publish a rival newspaper in the Riverland area. This led both parties to come to an arrangement that saw each newspaper restrict its circulation to the original locales. Various competition law breaches were alleged, including that there was the making and giving effect to an anticompetitive agreement. It was held that the arrangement had the purpose and effect of substantially lessening competition in the Murray Bridge regional newspaper market. Evidence that supported this included examples of advertisers moving from one newspaper to another, the close attention paid by the directors of Waikerie to the threat made by Rural Press, and the wider range of news that was available when two newspapers were competing with each other.

A. Price Fixing

178. Price fixing is primarily governed by Division 1 of Part IV of the CCA. This provision also deals with output restrictions, customer and territory allocation, as well as bid-rigging. The key provision is section 45AD (noted above).

179. The key focus under this legislation as far as price-fixing is concerned (the remaining elements such as purpose, effect and parties being in competition with each other are common to competition law generally) is how fixing, controlling or maintaining of prices will be identified. The courts have recognized that this is not used in any technical sense.[153] The ordinary dictionary meaning of 'make fast, firm or stable' is what is intended.[154] For a person to be found guilty of price-fixing, they must have relinquished their independent decision-making powers.[155] The purpose

152. (2003) 216 CLR 53.
153. *Apco Service Stations Pty Ltd v. ACCC* [2005] ATPR 42-078.
154. *Apco Service Stations Pty Ltd v. ACCC* [2005] ATPR 42-078, [44].
155. *Apco Service Stations Pty Ltd v. ACCC* [2005] ATPR 42-078.

required under this legislation is the subjective purpose.[156] The competition condition identified in section 44ZZRD(1)(b) is met by the following legislative test:

> Once the definition requirements are met, a corporation will commit an offence if they make a contract, an arrangement or understanding that contains a cartel provision. An offence also results if a corporation gives effect to a cartel provision (section 45AG). These offences can also constitute what are known as civil penalty provisions (sections 45AJff). There are a number of exceptions (*see* subdivision D of Division 1 of Part IV – these include where there is a collective bargaining notice in force, there is a grant of authorization, the conduct is between related bodies corporate, joint ventures, covenants affecting competition, resale price maintenance, exclusive dealing, dual listed company arrangements or mergers). For the corporation, civil penalties can reach a maximum of AUD 10,000,000, three times the benefit obtained, or if this is not possible, 10% of the turnover in the twelve months prior to the commission. Where criminal sanctions are sought against a natural person, gaol terms can reach to ten years and/or a fine not exceeding 2,000 penalty units. For a criminal sanction, the prosecution must establish the matter beyond a reasonable doubt. For civil matters, it will need to be proven on the balance of probabilities. An example of price fixing (under the previous legislation) is *ACCC v. Leahy Petroleum*.[157] The regulator brought an action against a number of petrol service station operators. The ACCC relied on the circumstantial evidence that prices rose after a number of telephone calls were made and/or received by the retailers. The Full Federal Court held that as, one party at least, did not commit to the proposed price increases and retained their capacity to make an independent decision, there was no price fixing. Another illustration can also be seen in *Radio 2UE Sydney Pty Ltd v. Stereo FM Pty Ltd*.[158] Stereo FM (a radio station) entered into an agreement with another radio station where they joined together to provide a combined advertising rate card, enabling advertising agencies to book advertising on both stations. The rate charged was a combination of the individual charges set by each station. Revenue was divided according to the share of the combined card. Radio 2UE (a competing station) sought an injunction to prevent the use of the combined advertising card. The basis was that its use contravened section 45 of the CCA. It was held that there was no price fixing. Each party was able to set their own prices – there was no element of making firm or stable the rates to be charged.

156. *ASX Operations Pty Ltd v. Pont Data Australian Pty Ltd (No. 2)* (1991) 27 FCR 492.
157. [2005] ATPR 42-078.
158. (1982) 2 TPR 315.

B. *Market/Client Allocation*

180. Market/client allocation is dealt with in Division 1 of Part IV of the CCA. Market/client allocation can occur where competitors divide customers along geographical areas, or where there is an agreement not to compete, or an agreement not to expand into another area.

C. *Product/Innovation Limitation*

181. The closest parallel to this in Australia would be output restrictions. An example of this is where an industry association work with its members to deliberately dampen supply, and thus reduce future price declines.[159]

D. *Group Boycotts*

182. In Australia, primary boycotts are considered under, either, division 1 or division 2 of Part IV (considered above). Secondary boycotts are considered under section 45D of the CCA.

Secondary Boycotts

183. Section 45D provides:

1. In the circumstances specified in subsection (3) or (4), a person must not, in concert with a second person, engage in conduct:
   a. that hinders or prevents:
      – a third person supplying goods or services to a fourth person (who is not an employer of the first person or the second person); or
      – a third person acquiring goods or services from a fourth person (who is not an employer of the first person or the second person); and
   b. that is engaged in for the purpose, and would have or be likely to have the effect, of causing substantial loss or damage to the business of the fourth person.
2. Note 1: Conduct that would otherwise contravene this section can be authorised under subsection 88
3. Note 2: This section also has effect subject to section 45DD, which deals with permitted boycotts.
4. A person is taken to engage in conduct for a purpose mentioned in subsection (1) if the person engages in the conduct for purposes that include that purpose.
5. Subsection (1) applies if the fourth person is a corporation.

159. For illustrations see ACCC, *Cartels – What You Need to Know, a Guide for Business* (Canberra, 2012), 12; see http://www.accc.gov.au/business/anti-competitive-behaviour/cartels.

6. Subsection (1) also applies if:
   a. the third person is a corporation and the fourth person is not a corporation; and
   b. the conduct would have or be likely to have the effect of causing substantial loss or damage to the business of the third person.

184. Intractably connected to section 45D are sections 45DA, DB and E. Section 45DA prohibits two persons acting in concert from hindering or preventing a third person trading with a fourth person (the target) where the purpose and effect (or likely effect) of the conduct is to cause a substantial lessening of competition in any market in which the fourth person supplies or acquires goods or services. Section 45DB relates specifically to the movement of goods between Australia and places outside Australia. Section 45E relates to the supply or acquisition of goods and services. Remedies available for contravention of section 45D include, for the Commission:

– pecuniary penalties of up to AUD 750,000 for a corporation (individuals are not liable to pecuniary penalties under section 45D);
– injunctions; and
– ancillary orders.

185. Individuals may apply to the court for:

– injunctions;
– damages; and
– ancillary orders.

186. Authorization immunity is available for section 45D practices under section 88 of the CCA.

187. The central issue to note with respect to this provision is that unlike the other substantial lessening of competition provisions in the CCA, section 45D does not give the plaintiff the option of proving either an anticompetitive purpose or an anticompetitive effect: to satisfy this provision, both purpose and effect must be established. An example of the operation of this provision is *Australasian Meat Industry Employees Union & Ors v. Mudginberri Station Pty Ltd.*[160] The facts as described by Morling J. were as follows (at 47, 750):

> On 9 May 1985 the applicant commenced its operations at Mudginberri for the 1985 season. The following day the picket line was established and has since been maintained. ... The effect of the picket line was to shut down the applicant's export operations ... causing the applicant substantial losses. Meat may not be exported unless it has first been inspected by appropriately qualified meat inspectors. It is the responsibility of the Department of Primary Industry to allocate inspectors to the Mudginberri abattoir. Three meat inspectors have

160. (1986) ATPR 40-709.

> been assigned to it. ... [T]he inspectors have declined to cross the picket line [having been told that], if necessary, physical force would be used to prevent inspectors working if they crossed the picket line. There is also evidence ... that the transport of goods to the abattoir has been impeded because of the picket line. In the last few weeks the applicant has been able to carry on limited operations at the abattoir by producing meat for the domestic market, but I am satisfied that it is still suffering continuing loss and damage to its business.

188. His Honour was satisfied that a breach of section 45D had been established. The union and the employees had worked in concert together to prevent the meat inspectors from crossing the picket line, and that conduct had both the purpose and the effect of causing substantial loss to the business of the applicant. Recommendation 36 of the Australian Government, *Review of Competition Policy Final Report* (March, 2015) is to the effect that the secondary boycott provisions, which have rarely been used, should be maintained and enforced with 'increased vigour'.[161]

E. Collusion on Other Objects

In Australia, collusive practices would come within the practices previously outlined.

II. Information Exchange Practices

189. There is no direct prohibition against competitors exchanging information. However, a cautionary tale must be noted that such a practice would invariably come under close examination. In *Trade Practices Commission v. Email*,[162] the defendant and another entity Warburton Franki were the only two manufacturers of electricity meters in Australia. They routinely exchanged price lists, submitted identical tenders and otherwise passed on price information. Email was the undisputed market leader in the country. Perhaps surprisingly, no breach of section 45 was established. The role of Email as market leader was critical to this finding. If Warburton Franki had not followed the pricing of Email, it is possible that it would have been driven out of business.

161. Recent illustrations of the use of s. 45D, though not directly involving the regulator, include *Boral Resources (Vic) Pty Ltd v. Construction, Forestry, Mining and Energy Union* [2014] VSC 429; *Ralan St Leonards Pty Ltd v. Construction, Forestry, Mining and Energy Union* [2014] FCA 431.
162. (1980) 43 FLR 383.

III. Cooperation Agreements

190. The control and regulation of cooperation agreements or as they are more likely to be known in Australia, joint ventures, is heavily regulated by statute. A joint venture is defined as follows:

> In this Act:
>
> (a) a reference to a joint venture is a reference to an activity in trade or commerce:
>   (i) carried on jointly by two or more persons, whether or not in partnership; or
>   (ii) carried on by a body corporate formed by two or more persons for the purpose of enabling those persons to carry on that activity jointly by means of their joint control, or by means of their ownership of shares in the capital, of that body corporate; and
>
> (b) a reference to a contract or arrangement made or understanding arrived at, or to a proposed contract or arrangement to be made or proposed understanding to be arrived at, for the purposes of a joint venture shall, in relation to a joint venture by way of an activity carried on by a body corporate as mentioned in subparagraph(a)(ii), be read as including a reference to the memorandum and articles of association, rules or other document that constitute or constitutes, or are or is to constitute, that body corporate.

191. As is recognized under competition law, joint ventures can be pro-competitive or anticompetitive. Critically, in determining whether the joint venture will fall foul of the CCA is consideration of what is the underlying substance of the agreement. On the one hand, it may be considered simply as a merger and falls for evaluation under those provisions (section 50). Contrastingly, it may simply be seen as two competitors working together to control price or output in a particular market – this is a breach of the substantive provisions such as section 45. However, the two entities may well establish a relationship to enter a new market, or put out into the market place a product that neither could do on their own. In this context, the joint venture may be seen as pro-competitive. Because of these conflicting issues, the legislation provides a number of specific opportunities for those within a joint venture to establish a defence to what would otherwise be a breach of the legislation. For example, section 45AO and 45AP of the CCA provides a response to an allegation that an arrangement between two parties involves a breach of the legislation. It states:

> 45AO Joint ventures – prosecution
> Sections 45AF and 45AG do not apply in relation to a contract, arrangement or understanding containing a cartel provision if the defendant proves that:
>
> (a) the cartel provision is:
>   (i) for the purposes of a joint venture; and
>   (ii) reasonably necessary for undertaking the joint venture; and

(b) the joint venture is for any one or more of the following:
   (i) production of goods;
   (ii) supply of goods or services;
   (iii) acquisition of goods or services; and
(c) the joint venture is not carried on for the purpose of substantially lessening competition; and
(d) in a case where subparagraph4J(a)(i) applies to the joint venture—the joint venture is carried on jointly by the parties to the contract, arrangement or understanding; and
(e) in a case where subparagraph4J(a)(ii) applies to the joint venture the joint venture is carried on by a body corporate formed by the parties to the contract, arrangement or understanding for the purpose of enabling those parties to carry on the activity mentioned in paragraph(b) jointly by means of:
   (i) their joint control; or
   (ii) their ownership of shares in the capital;
   of that body corporate.

Note 1: A defendant bears a legal burden in relation to the matter in this section (see section 13.4 of the *Criminal Code*).
Note 2: For example, if a joint venture formed for the purpose of research and development provides the results of its research and development to participants in the joint venture, it may be a joint venture for the supply of services.

45AP Joint ventures – civil penalty proceedings

(1) Sections 45AJ and 45AK do not apply in relation to a contract, arrangement or understanding containing a cartel provision if the defendant proves that:
   (a) the cartel provision is:
      (i) for the purposes of a joint venture; and
      (ii) reasonably necessary for undertaking the joint venture; and
   (b) the joint venture is for any one or more of the following:
      (i) production of goods;
      (ii) supply of goods or services;
      (iii) acquisition of goods or services; and
   (c) the joint venture is not carried on for the purpose of substantially lessening competition; and
   (d) in a case where subparagraph 4J(a)(i) applies to the joint venture—the joint venture is carried on jointly by the parties to the contract, arrangement or understanding; and
   (e) in a case where subparagraph 4J(a)(ii) applies to the joint venture—the joint venture is carried on by a body corporate formed by the parties to the contract, arrangement or understanding for the purpose of enabling those parties to carry on the activity mentioned in paragraph (b) jointly by means of:
      (i) their joint control; or
      (ii) their ownership of shares in the capital;
      of that body corporate.

Note: For example, if a joint venture formed for the purpose of research and development provides the results of its research and development to participants in the joint venture, it may be a joint venture for the supply of services.

(2) A defendant who wishes to rely on subsection (1) must prove that matter on the balance of probabilities.

A. Research and Development

192. Research and development joint ventures will fall for consideration under the principles highlighted above.

B. Specialization

193. Joint ventures that lead to further specialization will fall for consideration under the principles highlighted above.

C. Standardization

194. Joint ventures that lead to industry standardization will fall for consideration under the principles highlighted above.

D. Joint Production

195. The regulator has largely endorsed joint production ventures as pro-competitive. In some of the scenarios where this has been permitted, the venture to be undertaken has involved large resources with an expensive upfront capital outlay, such as in mineral exploration.[163]

E. Joint Purchasing

196. Joint purchasing ventures will fall for consideration under the elements highlighted above.

---

163. See generally S. Corones, *Competition Law in Australia,* 6th edn (Sydney: Thomson Reuters., 2014), Ch. 6.

F. Joint Selling

197. It has been suggested that marketing joint ventures are likely to face scrutiny.[164] They will often be seen as two competitors colluding, rather than independently competing.

§2. Vertical Agreements

198. In Australia, two types of vertical agreements are regulated. These are exclusive dealing (section 47) and resale price maintenance (section 48). Resale price maintenance is considered in this initial overview, and consideration of exclusive dealing will then follow.

199. Section 48 prohibits the practice of resale price maintenance (RPM). Simply stated, it says that a corporation or other person shall not engage in the practice of resale price maintenance. However, the details of this provision can be found, rather unusually, much later in the legislation. As to what constitutes resale price maintenance, section 96(3) provides the answer:

> 96(3) The acts referred to in subsections (1) and (2) are the following:
>
> a. the supplier making it known to a second person that the supplier will not supply goods to the second person unless the second person agrees not to sell those goods at a price less than a price specified by the supplier;
> b. the supplier inducing, or attempting to induce, a second person not to sell, at a price less than a price specified by the supplier, goods supplied to the second person by the supplier or by a third person who, directly or indirectly, has obtained the goods from the supplier;
> c. the supplier entering into an agreement, or offering to enter into an agreement, for the supply of goods to a second person, being an agreement one of the terms of which is, or would be, that the second person will not sell the goods at a price less than a price specified, or that would be specified, by the supplier;
> d. the supplier withholding the supply of goods to a second person for the reason that the second person:
>   – has not agreed as mentioned in paragraph (a); or
>   – has sold, or is likely to sell, goods supplied to him or her by the supplier, or goods supplied to him or her by a third person who, directly or indirectly, has obtained the goods from the supplier, at a price less than a price specified by the supplier as the price below which the goods are not to be sold;
> e. the supplier withholding the supply of goods to a second person for the reason that a third person who, directly or indirectly, has obtained, or wishes to obtain, goods from the second person:

164. S. Corones, *Competition Law in Australia*, 6th edn (Sydney: Thomson Reuters., 2014), Ch. 6.

  - has not agreed not to sell those goods at a price less than a price specified by the supplier; or
  - has sold, or is likely to sell, goods supplied to him or her, or to be supplied to him or her, by the second person, at a price less than a price specified by the supplier as the price below which the goods are not to be sold; and

f. the supplier using, in relation to any goods supplied, or that may be supplied, by the supplier to a second person, a statement of a price that is likely to be understood by that person as the price below which the goods are not to be sold.

200. This legislation relates to minimum prices, and there is no prohibition in section 48 on the setting of maximum prices. Despite the detail in the legislation, in essence what it does is prohibit a supplier of goods from establishing the price that they are to be sold at by the retailer. It is also known as vertical price-fixing, whereby the wholesaler or supplier is seeking to impose restrictions on the independent decision-making of the retailer. For an outline of the civil remedies available to the ACCC.

201. As with the other provisions, individuals may apply to the court for injunctions, damages or ancillary orders.

202. It is possible to obtain authorization or notification of resale price maintenance (section 88).

203. The legislation goes on to provide in sections 97–100 that:

- Recommended prices will not breach the legislation (section 97).
- The circumstances in which there is a withholding of supply are set out in section 98.
- As to what constitutes a minimum price, consideration is had to section 99. This indicates that a statement woven or affixed to goods, a statement used in a sign, invoice, catalogue or advertising or a statement which appears on a covering label or package, or any other document which appears to refer to certain goods or services will constitute reference to the minimum price.
- Section 100 provides a number of presumptions that will assist in establishing resale price maintenance at the practical level. In effect, it operates to reverse the onus of proof. It provides that where the supplier has withheld supply after becoming aware that the retailer has been discounting the product within the last six months, the supplier bears the onus of establishing that they did not breach the resale price maintenance provisions.

204. Resale price maintenance can also apply in relation to services. Section 96A states:

96A Resale price maintenance in relation to services

1. This Part applies to conduct in relation to services in a way that corresponds to the way it applies to conduct in relation to goods.
2. For the purposes of subsection (1), this Part is to be read with appropriate modifications, including the following modifications:
   a. references in this Part to goods are to be read as references to services;
   b. references to the sale of goods are to be read as references to the re-supply of services.

205. An example of resale price maintenance can be seen in *ACCC v. Dermalogica Pty Ltd.*[165] Dermalogica wished to promote its products as a premium brand. When online sites began advertising at a price of 10% below the recommended price, the defendant approached the retailers and advised them that their accounts would be closed if they did not cease discounting. They sought to argue that they had not engaged in resale price maintenance in violation of section 96(3)(a) in that they had not indicated with complete finality that there would be a withholding unless the recommended price was adhered to. The Court rejected this. 'The supplier might make the threat even though it well knew that it was impossible or highly unlikely that it would act upon the threat.'[166]

206. Resale price maintenance is unique when compared with the other competition law provisions. This offence has the specific defence of 'loss leader'. This is created by section 98(2–3). This provides:

1. Paragraph 96(3)(d) does not apply in relation to the withholding by the supplier of the supply of goods to another person who, within the preceding year, has sold goods obtained, directly or indirectly, from the supplier at less than their cost to that other person:
   a. for the purpose of attracting to the establishment at which the goods were sold persons likely to purchase other goods; or
   b. otherwise for the purpose of promoting the business of that other person.
2. For the purposes of subsection (2), there shall be disregarded:
   a. a genuine seasonal or clearance sale of goods that were not acquired for the purpose of being sold at that sale; or
   b. a sale of goods that took place with the consent of the supplier.

207. In effect, it allows a supplier to refuse supply where the retailer is merely using the discounted goods to attract customers into the shop – presumably with the intent to buy other items. This defence cannot be used where there is a genuine clearance sale in relation to the items. A successful application of this defence can be seen in *Kadkhudayan v. WD & HO Wills (Australia) Limited.*[167] Wills had refused to continue to supply the applicant when the applicant was selling below

165. (2005) 215 ALR 482.
166. (2005) 215 ALR 482, [48]. See also *Australian Competition and Consumer Commission v. Eternal Beauty Products Pty Ltd* [2012] FCA 1124; *Australian Competition and Consumer Commission (ACCC) v. Mitsubishi Electric Australia Pty Ltd* [2013] FCA 1413.
167. [2001] ATPR 41-822.

the wholesale price specified by Wills. Various promotion payments were withheld from Kadkhudayan in an effort to bring him into line. Wills successfully argued loss leader – the applicant was merely using low-cost cigarettes as a means to bring people into his shop.

I. Distribution

A. Exclusive Distributorship

This would fall for consideration under principles relating to exclusive dealing – see the following paragraphs.

B. Exclusive Dealing

208. Section 47, though technical in its approach, has at its heart, the conditional prohibition on a supplier directly or indirectly interfering with the freedom of buyers to buy from or to sell to whom they choose. Similarly, buyers are conditionally prohibited from imposing restrictions on the freedom of supplies to sell as they wish. Such exclusive dealing practices are illegal under section 47 if they have the purpose, effect or likely effect of substantially lessening competition.

209. Given the technical nature of the legislation, it is necessary to repeat the legislation in its entirety:

47 Exclusive dealing

(1) Subject to this section, a corporation shall not, in trade or commerce, engage in the practice of exclusive dealing.

(2) A corporation engages in the practice of exclusive dealing if the corporation:

(a) supplies, or offers to supply, goods or services;

(b) supplies, or offers to supply, goods or services at a particular price; or

(c) gives or allows, or offers to give or allow, a discount, allowance, rebate or credit in relation to the supply or proposed supply of goods or services by the corporation;

on the condition that the person to whom the corporation supplies, or offers or proposes to supply, the goods or services or, if that person is a body corporate, a body corporate related to that body corporate:

(d) will not, or will not except to a limited extent, acquire goods or services, or goods or services of a particular kind or description, directly or indirectly from a competitor of the corporation or from a competitor of a body corporate related to the corporation;

(e) will not, or will not except to a limited extent, re-supply goods or services, or goods or services of a particular kind or description, acquired directly or indirectly from a competitor of the corporation or from a competitor of a body corporate related to the corporation; or

(f) in the case where the corporation supplies or would supply goods or services, will not re-supply the goods or services to any person, or will not, or will not except to a limited extent, re-supply the goods or services:

(i) to particular persons or classes of persons or to persons other than particular persons or classes of persons; or

(ii) in particular places or classes of places or in places other than particular places or classes of places.

(3) A corporation also engages in the practice of exclusive dealing if the corporation refuses:

(a) to supply goods or services to a person;

(b) to supply goods or services to a person at a particular price; or

(c) to give or allow a discount, allowance, rebate or credit in relation to the supply or proposed supply of goods or services to a person;

for the reason that the person or, if the person is a body corporate, a body corporate related to that body corporate:

(d) has acquired, or has not agreed not to acquire, goods or services, or goods or services of a particular kind or description, directly or indirectly from a competitor of the corporation or from a competitor of a body corporate related to the corporation;

(e) has re-supplied, or has not agreed not to re-supply, goods or services, or goods or services of a particular kind or description, acquired directly or indirectly from a competitor of the corporation or from a competitor of a body corporate related to the corporation; or

(f) has re-supplied, or has not agreed not to re-supply, goods or services, or goods or services of a particular kind or description, acquired from the corporation to any person, or has re-supplied, or has not agreed not to re-supply, goods or services, or goods or services of a particular kind or description, acquired from the corporation:

(i) to particular persons or classes of persons or to persons other than particular persons or classes of persons; or

(ii) in particular places or classes of places or in places other than particular places or classes of places.

(4) A corporation also engages in the practice of exclusive dealing if the corporation:

(a) acquires, or offers to acquire, goods or services; or

(b) acquires, or offers to acquire, goods or services at a particular price;

on the condition that the person from whom the corporation acquires or offers to acquire the goods or services or, if that person is a body corporate, a body corporate related to that body corporate will not supply goods or services, or goods or services of a particular kind or description, to any person, or will not, or will not except to a limited extent, supply goods or services, or goods or services of a particular kind or description:

(c) to particular persons or classes of persons or to persons other than particular persons or classes of persons; or
(d) in particular places or classes of places or in places other than particular places or classes of places.

(5) A corporation also engages in the practice of exclusive dealing if the corporation refuses:
(a) to acquire goods or services from a person; or
(b) to acquire goods or services at a particular price from a person;

for the reason that the person or, if the person is a body corporate, a body corporate related to that body corporate has supplied, or has not agreed not to supply, goods or services, or goods or services of a particular kind or description:
(c) to particular persons or classes of persons or to persons other than particular persons or classes of persons; or
(d) in particular places or classes of places or in places other than particular places or classes of places.

(6) A corporation also engages in the practice of exclusive dealing if the corporation:
(a) supplies, or offers to supply, goods or services;
(b) supplies, or offers to supply, goods or services at a particular price; or
(c) gives or allows, or offers to give or allow, a discount, allowance, rebate or credit in relation to the supply or proposed supply of goods or services by the corporation;

on the condition that the person to whom the corporation supplies or offers or proposes to supply the goods or services or, if that person is a body corporate, a body corporate related to that body corporate will acquire goods or services of a particular kind or description directly or indirectly from another person not being a body corporate related to the corporation.

(7) A corporation also engages in the practice of exclusive dealing if the corporation refuses:
(a) to supply goods or services to a person;
(b) to supply goods or services at a particular price to a person; or
(c) to give or allow a discount, allowance, rebate or credit in relation to the supply of goods or services to a person;

for the reason that the person or, if the person is a body corporate, a body corporate related to that body corporate has not acquired, or has not agreed to acquire, goods or services of a particular kind or description directly or indirectly from another person not being a body corporate related to the corporation.

(8) A corporation also engages in the practice of exclusive dealing if the corporation grants or renews, or makes it known that it will not exercise a power or right to terminate, a lease of, or a licence in respect of, land or a building or part of a building on the condition that another party to the lease or licence or, if that other party is a body corporate, a body corporate related to that body corporate:
(a) will not, or will not except to a limited extent:

(i) acquire goods or services, or goods or services of a particular kind or description, directly or indirectly from a competitor of the corporation or from a competitor of a body corporate related to the corporation; or

(ii) re-supply goods or services, or goods or services of a particular kind or description, acquired directly or indirectly from a competitor of the corporation or from a competitor of a body corporate related to the corporation;

(b) will not supply goods or services, or goods or services of a particular kind or description, to any person, or will not, or will not except to a limited extent, supply goods or services, or goods or services of a particular kind or description:

(i) to particular persons or classes of persons or to persons other than particular persons or classes of persons; or

(ii) in particular places or classes of places or in places other than particular places or classes of places; or

(c) will acquire goods or services of a particular kind or description directly or indirectly from another person not being a body corporate related to the corporation.

(9) A corporation also engages in the practice of exclusive dealing if the corporation refuses to grant or renew, or exercises a power or right to terminate, a lease of, or a licence in respect of, land or a building or part of a building for the reason that another party to the lease or licence or, if that other party is a body corporate, a body corporate related to that body corporate:

(a) has acquired, or has not agreed not to acquire, goods or services, or goods or services of a particular kind or description, directly or indirectly from a competitor of the corporation or from a competitor of a body corporate related to the corporation;

(b) has re-supplied, or has not agreed not to re-supply, goods or services, or goods or services of a particular kind or description, acquired directly or indirectly from a competitor of the corporation or from a competitor of a body corporate related to the corporation;

(c) has supplied goods or services, or goods or services of a particular kind or description:

(i) to particular persons or classes of persons or to persons other than particular persons or classes of persons; or

(ii) in particular places or classes of places or in places other than particular places or classes of places; or

(d) has not acquired, or has not agreed to acquire, goods or services of a particular kind or description directly or indirectly from another person not being a body corporate related to the corporation.

(10) Subsection (1) does not apply to the practice of exclusive dealing by a corporation unless:

(a) the engaging by the corporation in the conduct that constitutes the practice of exclusive dealing has the purpose, or has or is likely to have the effect, of substantially lessening competition; or

(b) the engaging by the corporation in the conduct that constitutes the practice of exclusive dealing, and the engaging by the corporation, or by a body corporate related to the corporation, in other conduct of the same or a similar kind, together have or are likely to have the effect of substantially lessening competition.

(11) Subsections (8) and (9) do not apply with respect to:
(a) conduct engaged in:
(i) by a registered charity; and
(ii) for or in accordance with the purposes or objects of that registered charity; or
(b) conduct engaged in in pursuance of a legally enforceable requirement made by a registered charity, being a requirement made for or in accordance with the purposes or objects of that registered charity.

(12) Subsection (1) does not apply with respect to any conduct engaged in by a body corporate by way of restricting dealings by another body corporate if those bodies corporate are related to each other.

(13) In this section:
(a) a reference to a condition shall be read as a reference to any condition, whether direct or indirect and whether having legal or equitable force or not, and includes a reference to a condition the existence or nature of which is ascertainable only by inference from the conduct of persons or from other relevant circumstances;
(b) a reference to competition, in relation to conduct to which a provision of this section other than subsection (8) or (9) applies, shall be read as a reference to competition in any market in which:
(i) the corporation engaging in the conduct or any body corporate related to that corporation; or
(ii) any person whose business dealings are restricted, limited or otherwise circumscribed by the conduct or, if that person is a body corporate, any body corporate related to that body corporate;
supplies or acquires, or is likely to supply or acquire, goods or services or would, but for the conduct, supply or acquire, or be likely to supply or acquire, goods or services; and
(c) a reference to competition, in relation to conduct to which subsection (8) or (9) applies, shall be read as a reference to competition in any market in which the corporation engaging in the conduct or any other corporation the business dealings of which are restricted, limited or otherwise circumscribed by the conduct, or any body corporate related to either of those corporations, supplies or acquires, or is likely to supply or acquire, goods or services or would, but for the conduct, supply or acquire, or be likely to supply or acquire, goods or services.

The remedies available to the ACCC are as detailed above. If there is a delay in providing assistance to the ACCC, the penalty imposed can be higher.[168]

168. *Australian Competition and Consumer Commission v Oakmoore Pty Ltd* [2018] FCA 1472.

Individuals may apply to the court for the usual remedies of an injunction, damages and associated ancillary orders.

It is possible to obtain notification immunity under section 95 for section 47 exclusive dealing practices. Under section 88 of the legislation, exclusive dealing can also be authorized.

A taxonomy to approach an understanding of exclusive dealing can be given as follows:

- Product restrictions
- Customer restrictions
- Territorial restrictions.

210. In *ACCC v. Fila Sport Oceania Pty Ltd*,[169] Fila was licensed by the Australian Football League (AFL) to supply clothing to the teams within the AFL. There were two types of clothing. One was on-field clothing that was the same as that worn by the players. The other category was 'team-spirit' clothing. This type of clothing would feature the team logo or team colours. Many additional manufacturers were licensed to produce 'team-spirit' clothing. However, this was not the case with on-field clothing – a small number had exclusive licenses. Fila was also a direct sponsor of a number of teams in the competition. Fila introduced a selective distribution policy that prevented a retailer from stocking team-spirit clothing licensed by another manufacturer – particularly in respect of teams that were sponsored by Fila. This was held to be exclusive dealing (section 47(2)(d)). An example of a territorial restriction can be seen in *Mark Lyons Pty Ltd v. Bursill Sportsgear Pty Ltd.*[170] The defendant had refused to supply in circumstances where Mark Lyons Pty Ltd refused to commit to a restriction on supply in certain places, such as warehouses and town halls.

C. Selective Distributorship

211. This would fall for consideration under exclusive dealing. For example, the case of *ACCC v. Fila Sport Oceania Pty Ltd*[171] could also be considered an example of selective distributorship.

D. Franchising

212. In Australia, three types of franchises have been recognized. These include:

- a product franchise whereby the manufacturer provides an exclusive (probably territorial) arrangement for the distribution of its products. An example is a franchise for the retail sale of motor vehicles;

169. [2004] ATPR 41-983.
170. (1987) 75 ALR 581.
171. [2004] ATPR 41-983.

- a processing franchise whereby a manufacturer provides the know-how to another entity permitting them to produce the item in question. An example is in the soft-drink industry;
- a business system franchise whereby the franchisor develops a unique way to develop a good or service and permits the franchisee to deliver that item in accordance with that system. The most obvious examples are in the fast food outlets, the exemplar being McDonalds.[172]

213. Cases directly considering franchises in Australia are rare, though on occasions, franchises have sought to obtain either authorization or notification of the franchise agreement. For example, Coca-Cola was successful in receiving notification for an exclusive territorial franchise, the Commission satisfied that while there were some restrictions on intra-brand competition, there was little overall anticompetitive effect.[173] This reasoning flowed from the lack of complaints about the exclusive arrangements and the presence of inter-brand competition.

II. Intellectual Property Licensing

A. Patent

214. Until recently, section 51 of the CCA provided a limited exemption for intellectual property dealings from the operation of certain Part IV provisions. This exemption effectively insulated certain terms and conditions in intellectual property licences from contravening particular Part IV provisions. The provision was repealed in September 2019. At the time of writing, the ACCC has undertaken to produce guidelines to assist intellectual property holders in avoiding contraventions of Part IV provisions.

215. The High Court has also recognized that section 46 of the CCA (misuse of market power) may be used to order the compulsory licensing of intellectual property rights.[174]

B. Trademarks Licensing

216. See directly above.

---

172. These three forms were identified by the Swanson Committee, 'Competition and Consumer Act Review Committee', *Report to the Minister for Business and Consumer Affairs,* AGPS (Canberra, 1976), para. 5.2.
173. [1978] ATPR (Com) 35-400.
174. *NT Power Generation v. Power and Water Authority* (2004) 219 CLR 90, [125].

C. Know-How Trade Secret Licensing

217. Non-statutory confidential information would fall for consideration under the legislative principles relevant to Part IV of the CCA. There is no specific statutory protection or exemption for know-how trade secret licensing.

Chapter 2. Dominant Undertakings' Prohibited Practices

218. Section 46 of the CCA prohibits the misuse of market power. The section applies to unilateral conduct. The section prevents a firm from engaging in conduct in which it could not engage in a competitive market. Section 46 provides:

> (1) A corporation that has a substantial degree of power in a market must not engage in conduct that has the purpose, or has or is likely to have the effect, of substantially lessening competition in:
> (a) that market; or
> (b) any other market in which that corporation, or a body corporate that is related to that corporation:
> (i) supplies goods or services, or is likely to supply goods or services; or
> (ii) supplies goods or services, or is likely to supply goods or services, indirectly through one or more other persons; or
> (c) any other market in which that corporation, or a body corporate that is related to that corporation:
> (i) acquires goods or services, or is likely to acquire goods or services; or
> (ii) acquires goods or services, or is likely to acquire goods or services, indirectly through one or more other persons.

219. From this statutory definition, the elements required to be proved in establishing the offence are:

- the corporation must have substantial market power in a relevant market;
- it must engage in conduct; and
- the purpose, effect or likely effect of that conduct is to substantially lessen competition in a market.

220. The primary objective of section 46 is the promotion of competition in order to protect consumers.[175] Thus, the section is concerned with economic rather than moral objectives in that it does not protect the private interests of individual persons or corporations.[176] In the achievement of this objective, competitors may be eliminated or damaged, but this is viewed as an inevitable consequence of the competition the section seeks to foster.[177] The focus on the protection of the competitive process means that small and medium-sized businesses are afforded no special protection.

221. Section 46A replicates section 46, but with a focus on the trans-Tasman market between Australia and New Zealand.

---

175. *Queensland Wire Industries Pty Ltd v. Broken Hill Proprietary Co Ltd* (1989) 167 CLR 177, 191–192.
176. *Melway Publishing Pty Ltd v. Robert Hicks Pty Ltd* (2001) 205 CLR 1, 13; *Boral Besser Masonry Ltd (now Boral Masonry Ltd) v. Australian Competition and Consumer Commission* (2003) 215 CLR 374, 411, 429, 459.
177. *Queensland Wire Industries Pty Ltd v. Broken Hill Proprietary Co Ltd* (1989) 167 CLR 177, 191.

§1. MARKET POWER

222. The first step in assessing market power is market definition. This is an important step in the evaluation of market power because the breadth of the defined market will determine whether market power is found to exist. The more broadly the market is defined, the less likely it is that a corporation will possess market power in that market. Section 46(1) also makes it clear that leveraging market power from one market to another will be caught by the prohibition in that a corporation with market power in a market must not engage in conduct that has the purpose or the effect of lessening competition in '... that or any other market'.[178]

223. Section 46, as initially enacted in 1974, required that a corporation be in a position to substantially control a market. There was a perception that section 46 needed to be more effective, in that the threshold of control meant that the section applied only to monopolists or those with overwhelming dominance in a market. In response to this concern, this threshold of 'substantial control' was reduced by virtue of the *Trade Practices Revision Act 1986* to the current 'substantial market power' standard.

224. As the threshold test in establishing a contravention of section 46, the assessment of market power is the first step in any evaluation under section 46. Market power must be considered prior to consideration of the other elements. The preliminary inquiry where liability under section 46 is in issue is the possession of substantial market power, and an examination of market power must occur outside the context of the impugned behaviour.[179] The conduct that is at issue should not be considered when market power is being assessed. This very structural approach to market power analysis raises a temporal issue. If consideration of market power must take place before consideration of the impugned conduct, strategic conduct undertaken with the aim of creating the ability to engage in anticompetitive conduct cannot be considered in assessing market power.[180]

225. Market power is an economic concept – therefore, the degree of market power is a legal question, but what constitutes market power is likely to be guided by economic evidence.

226. While early cases focused simply on market share in assessing market power[181] though there was no presumptive market power based on a threshold level of market share, more recent cases have taken a more expansive approach. The structural features of a market that need to be considered in making this assessment can be summarized as:

---

178. Section 46(1) *Competition and Consumer Act Competition and Consumer Act 2010* (Cth).
179. *Boral Besser Masonry Ltd (now Boral Masonry Ltd) v. Australian Competition and Consumer Commission* (2003) 195 ALR 609, 634.
180. *Boral Besser Masonry Ltd (now Boral Masonry Ltd) v. Australian Competition and Consumer Commission* (2003) 195 ALR 609, 693–694.
181. *Mark Lyons Pty Ltd v. Bursill Sportsgear Pty Ltd* (1987) 75 ALR 581.

- the degree of market concentration;
- the height of barriers to entry;
- the degree of product differentiation and sales promotion evident within the market;
- the nature of vertical relationships within the industry; and
- the nature of relationships between firms within the industry.[182]

227. References to 'power' within the context of section 46(1) should be taken to be references to market power and not some other kind of power. The possession of financial power will not, in itself, equate to market power.[183]

228. Market power has been described as the antithesis of competition or the ability to '... raise prices and exclude entry'.[184] Market power may, however, be exhibited by practices unrelated to price and is therefore defined more broadly than simply the ability to raise prices in an unconstrained manner.[185] It is commonly described as the ability to act persistently in a manner unconstrained by competition.[186] The ability to raise prices remains an important aspect of establishing market power, but it must be considered within the broader context of other relevant matters.[187] It must be asked whether the corporation can behave differently from the behaviour that a competitive market would enforce on that firm.[188]

229. In determining whether a corporation may act in an unconstrained manner, courts are required to have regard to the extent to which a corporation is free to determine its own conduct without being consistently inhibited from doing so by competitors, suppliers and customers.[189]

230. Barriers to entry have been consistently recognized as being one of the main indicators of market power and the presence or absence of competitive conditions.[190] There has been some recognition in recent Australian jurisprudence that strategic barriers to entry may be just as important as structural barriers to entry in assessing the ease of entry and the possession of market power.[191]

---

182. *Re Queensland Co-operative Milling Association Ltd v. Defiance Holdings Ltd* (1976) 25 FLR 169, 188.
183. *NT Power Generation Pty Ltd v. Power and Water Authority* (2004) 219 CLR 90 [115].
184. *Re Queensland Co-operative Milling Association Ltd v. Defiance Holdings Ltd* (1976) 25 FLR 169, 188.
185. *Queensland Wire Industries Pty Ltd v. Broken Hill Pty Co Ltd* (1989) 167 CLR 177, 200; *Re Queensland Co-operative Milling Association Ltd v. Defiance Holdings Ltd* (1976) 25 FLR 169, 188–189.
186. *Queensland Wire Industries Pty Ltd v. Broken Hill Pty Co Ltd* (1989) 167 CLR 177, 200.
187. *Queensland Wire Industries Pty Ltd v. Broken Hill Pty Co Ltd* (1989) 167 CLR 177.
188. *Queensland Wire Industries Pty Ltd v. Broken Hill Pty Co Ltd* (1989) 167 CLR 177.
189. Section 46(3) *Competition and Consumer Act 2010* (Cth).
190. *Queensland Wire Industries Pty Ltd v. Broken Hill Pty Co Ltd* (1989) 167 CLR 177.
191. *ACCC v. Boral Ltd* (2001) 106 FCR 328, 413; *Boral Besser Masonry Limited (now Boral Masonry Ltd) v. ACCC* (2003) 215 CLR 374, 478.

231. It is not enough for a firm to possess market power; that market power must be 'substantial'. Substantial in this context means 'considerable or large'.[192] The term is a relative concept and must be applied in respect of the circumstances of the particular case. So, for example, in *Australian Competition and Consumer Commission v. Pfizer Australian Pty Ltd*,[193] Pfizer held a patent on the atorvastatin molecule. This patent was about to expire. With the expiration of the patent looming, Pfizer instituted a direct-to-pharmacy business strategy that offered rebates and discounts to pharmacies in relation to the drug they produced (Lipitor) relating to the patent. Internal documents of Pfizer estimated that following the removal of the patent, sales of Lipitor would decline from some AUD 700 million in 2011, to AUD 70 million in 2015. The direct-to-pharmacy strategy was challenged by the ACCC on the basis that Pfizer's conduct was a misuse of market power in the Australian market for atorvastatin. The Full Court of the Federal Court found that the patent conferred substantial market power on Pfizer.[194] This substantial market power extended beyond the expiry of the patent because Pfizer was able to introduce its own generic version of the drug and to continue to supply Lipitor at the same price as that achieved prior to patent expiry. The claim failed as even though Pfizer did have substantial market power, and had taken advantage of that market power (as required by the legislation of the time), there was no evidence that they had used that power for a proscribed purpose (as also required by the legislation).[195] How these facts would play out in the current legislative framework where what needs to be established is the purpose, effect or likely effect of substantially lessening competition, is unclear.

232. It is now clear that a corporation may possess a substantial degree of power in a market despite the fact that it is not in a position to substantially control the market nor have absolute freedom from constraint.[196] More than one corporation may have substantial market power in a market.[197] Courts are not limited in what they may consider in assessing market power.[198] The market power of related bodies corporate may be considered in assessing market power,[199] although a shared position of market power with an unrelated corporation will not render a corporation liable.[200] Courts may, however, consider any contracts, arrangements or understandings the corporation has with other parties in assessing individual market power.[201] An example is provided by *Boral v. ACCC*.[202] Boral was held not to have substantial market power when it was found that it was the customers that were driving the price of concrete masonry products down, rather than their actions in

192. *Eastern Express Pty Limited v. General Newspapers Pty Ltd* (1992) 35 FCR 43, 46.
193. (2018) FCAFC 78.
194. (2018) FCAFC 78, [354]-[359].
195. (2018) FCAFC 78, [559]-[560].
196. Section 46(3C), *Competition and Consumer Act 2010* (Cth).
197. Section 46(3D), *Competition and Consumer Act 2010* (Cth).
198. Section 46(3B), *Competition and Consumer Act 2010* (Cth).
199. Section 46(2), *Competition and Consumer Act 2010* (Cth).
200. *Eastern Express Pty Ltd v. General Newspapers Pty Ltd* (1992) 35 FCR 43.
201. Section 46(3A), *Competition and Consumer Act 2010* (Cth).
202. (2003) 215 CLR 374.

competing with their competitors. This conclusion was reached by the High Court despite the market share of Boral growing from 28% to 42% during the relevant period. Supporting this conclusion was the fact that Boral could not have forced the prices of masonry products up.

§2. Engage in Conduct

233. A corporation with a substantial degree of power in a market must engage in conduct for the prohibition to be enlivened. The phrase 'engage in conduct' is not defined, though section 4F states:

> (b) a person shall be deemed to have engaged or to engage in conduct for a particular purpose or a particular reason if:
> (i) the person engaged or engages in the conduct for purposes that included or include that purpose or for reasons that included or include that reason, as the case may be; and
> (ii) that purpose or reason was or is a substantial purpose or reason.

§3. Purpose, Effect or Likely Effect of Substantially Lessening Competition

234. Section 46 will only be contravened if conduct has been engaged in, and the purpose, effect or likely effect is to substantially lessen competition. Paraphrased, the interim guidelines produced by the ACCC in relation to the effects test of section 46 provide the following points:[203]

- Purpose refers to a firm's intention to achieve a particular result;
- It must be a substantial purpose;
- Effect refers to the consequences of conduct;
- Effect is to be determined objectively;
- Evidence of consumer or competitive detriment will be relevant;
- Likely means something more possible than remotely;
- When assessing effect or likely effect, the ACCC will undertake a with, or without analysis. What is the state of affairs with the conduct – what is the state of affairs without the conduct;
- There is no definition of substantially lessening competition, but reliance can be had on the extant case law.[204]

203. ACCC, *Interim Guidelines on Misuse of Market Power,* October, 2017, pp7-9.
204. See also Julie Clarke 'Section 46: Its Purpose and the Proposed New Effects Test' (2017) 45 *Australian Business Law Review* 364.

§4. EXPLOITATIVE PRACTICES

I. Excessive/Unfair Pricing

235. Charging high or monopoly prices will not in itself contravene section 46(1). Corporations are entitled to reap the rewards of attaining market supremacy, and section 46(1) is not directed at monopolists merely exercising their market power.[205] This behaviour is likely to encourage competition. It is only where prices charged become excessive or unfair that section 46 may be contravened. This will only be the case where the charging of high prices is coupled with the purpose, or effect, or likely effect of substantially lessening competition.

236. In addition to section 46(1), Part VIIA of the CCA enables prices surveillance by the ACCC. This Part became effective on 1 March 2004. The object of Part VIIA is '... to have prices surveillance applied only in those markets where ... competitive pressures are not sufficient to achieve efficient prices and protect consumers'.[206] Part VIIA does two things. First, it provides for the ACCC to hold price inquiries in relation to the supply of particular goods or services.[207] These inquiries may relate to the supply of goods or services by a particular person[208] and may be at the instigation of the ACCC or the relevant Minister. If the ACCC determines that prices charged are excessive, it has the power to declare that a supplier is a declared supplier and that the goods or services in question are notified.[209] A declared supplier may not sell notified goods or services at a price higher than that in place over the previous twelve months, and a failure to adhere to the declaration will result in a fine.[210]

237. Second, Part VIIA allows the Minister for Competition Policy and Consumer Affairs, or the appropriate designated individual (currently the Assistant Minister to the Treasurer) to direct the ACCC to monitor prices, costs or profits relating to the supply of goods or services by persons in a specified industry. For example, the ACCC formally monitors the prices of unleaded petrol in cities and regional areas in Australia and can determine whether or not to object to proposed price increases.[211]

II. Discrimination

238. Some degree of price discrimination is permitted under the CCA. Like the charging of monopoly prices, discriminating in relation to prices charged to different groups of consumers may be efficiency-maximizing behaviour. It may not be the

205. *ASX Operations Pty Ltd v. Pont Data Australia Pty Ltd (No. 2)* (1991) 27 FCR 460.
206. Section 95E, *Competition and Consumer Act 2010* (Cth).
207. Section 95F(2), *Competition and Consumer Act 2010* (Cth).
208. Section 95F(3), *Competition and Consumer Act 2010* (Cth).
209. Section 95X, *Competition and Consumer Act 2010* (Cth).
210. Section 95Z, *Competition and Consumer Act 2010* (Cth).
211. See <www.accc.gov.au/content/index.phtml/itemId/142> viewed 30 Nov. 2009.

result of a corporation using its market power and indeed may not be as a result of that corporation possessing market power. Firms without market power may still engage in price discrimination, which ultimately benefits consumers if it results in more consumers being able to access the goods or services on offer.

239. Where, however, discriminatory prices can be charged because a corporation possesses market power, such price discrimination may contravene section 46(1). Price discrimination may take a number of forms, and there may be many ways in which anticompetitive price discrimination may be practised. For example, if the likely effect of the price discrimination was to substantially lessen competition then section 46 might be breached. Price discrimination, which operates to prevent suppliers from offering the same price to all buyers, may also contravene section 46(1). This will depend on the existence of market power (on the part of the buyer), and evidence of purpose, effect, or likely effect of substantially lessening competition.

§5. Exclusionary Practices

I. Predation

240. The term 'predatory pricing' is not used in the CCA. However, the term is generally understood under Australian competition law to mean selling below cost with intent to drive a competitor or competitors out of the market or generally reduce competition in the relevant market. As in other jurisdictions, the central issue will be whether the conduct is indeed predatory or simply competitive. While predatory pricing has long been considered to be unlawful under Australian competition law, courts have been reluctant to adopt the price-based tests traditionally used to assess the legality of predatory practices, and the High Court has specifically warned about imposing rigid rules relating to costs in imposing liability.[212]

II. Tying

241. Arrangements where a corporation with market power in one market offers some benefit to customers or suppliers, if they purchase other goods or services, may breach section 46(1). Bundling arrangements raise similar issues in respect of section 46. Where tying and bundling arrangements offer benefits to consumers, such as ensuring product quality and rewarding good customers, these arrangements will rarely contravene section 46. It is where market power is attained through leveraging into the tied market, or increased in the tied market, that section 46 may be contravened. It is crucial, however, that a purpose, effect, or likely effect of substantially lessening competition be found to exist before such contravention will be established. Tying or bundling may be restricted to one market, or it may

212. *Boral Besser Masonry Limited (now Boral Masonry Ltd) v. ACCC* (2003) 215 CLR 374, [128], [273].

reach across multiple markets. Section 46(1) would extend to such conduct provided it had the purpose, effect or likely effect, of substantially lessening competition.

III. Rebates

242. There are very few section 46(1) cases on point, however offering discounts and rebates will not, in most circumstances, contravene section 46 because they offer pro-competitive savings to customers and do not constitute something that would likely see a lessening of competition. This may not be the case where fidelity discounts require that customers acquire all or a substantial amount of their requirements in relation to a particular good, from the same supplier.

IV. Refusal to Deal

243. Generally, it is not a contravention of section 46 to refuse to deal. This is particularly the case where there is no history of dealing between parties. Different considerations will apply where there is a history of dealing between the parties, although there is surprisingly little Australian authority on point. The situation will also differ depending on whether the parties concerned are in a horizontal or vertical relationship, with vertical refusals to deal generally being viewed with more suspicion.

244. Section 46 may be used to gain access to assets that constitute essential facilities. A national access regime is contained in Part IIIA of the CCA. Part IIIA contains a procedure through which competitors may gain access to infrastructure facilities. Section 46 provides an alternative access regime, as the High Court confirmed in obiter in *NT Power Generation Pty Ltd v. Power and Water Authority*,[213] in stating that they did not view the existence of Part IIIA as precluding the parallel operation of section 46 as an access regime.[214] Section 46 may, therefore, be used to gain access to essential facilities. Section 46 operates in a manner comparable to the essential facilities doctrine in the US.[215]

245. The case of *NT Power Generation Pty Ltd v. Power and Water Authority*[216] demonstrates the way in how this access regime may be used. The PAWA was a government-owned electricity business, operating in the upstream (generation) and downstream (transmission, distribution and retail) market segments. A competitor in the generation market sought access to PAWA's transmission and distribution services so that its electricity could be managed by PAWA and sold by NT power in competition with PAWA. PAWA refused. The High Court rejected an argument

213. (2004) 219 CLR 90.
214. *NT Power Generation Pty Ltd v. Power and Water Authority* (2004) 219 CLR 90, [80]-[88].
215. Stephen Corones, *Competition Law in Australia*, 6th edn (Law book Co, 2014).
216. (2004) 219 CLR 90.

advanced by PAWA, based on previous legislation, that it was taking advantage of its proprietary rights rather than its market power and held that its proprietary rights gave rise to a substantial degree of market power.[217] It had taken advantage of this market power in refusing to manage NT Power's electricity. PAWA had effective control of the markets for the supply of services for the transmission and distribution of electricity, and if PAWA had been operating in a competitive market, it would be very unlikely that it would have stood by and let a competitor supply access services to NT Power.[218] It is likely the same result would occur under the current legislation, which demands attention to the question of whether there has been a lessening of competition.

246. There are no Australian cases dealing with refusals to licence intellectual property; however, section 46 theoretically provides an avenue for pursuing such an action.[219] Establishing a substantial degree of market power in such a case would be very difficult,[220] and there are likely to be many efficiency justifications for refusing to license intellectual property. Where supply to an existing licensee is discontinued, or licence terms made more onerous, an IP holder will have more difficulty in proving their conduct is efficient.[221]

V. Price Squeeze

247. Conduct that results in a price squeeze will usually contravene section 46. A successful section 46 action will be contingent on establishing that the upstream input is indeed essential and that the corporation engaging in the price squeeze has a substantial degree of market power.

248. A price squeeze occurred in *ASX Operations Pty Ltd v. Pont Data Australia Pty Ltd (No. 1)*,[222] where ASX Operations was held to have a substantial degree of market power in the two markets in which it operated. One of these markets was the market for supply of information and activities on stock exchanges. One division of ASX Operations supplied information to Pont Data. Another division competed with Pont Data in the retail market but was an inferior competitor to Pont Data's successful retail operation. In an effort to improve the operation of its retail section, a new agreement for the supply of information was entered into between ASX Operations and Pont Data. This increased price on a wholesale level and imposed restrictions on the use of the information and meant that Pont Data was unable to compete as successfully with ASX Operations at the retail level.

217. *NT Power Generation Pty Ltd v. Power and Water Authority* (2004) 219 CLR 90, [125].
218. *NT Power Generation Pty Ltd v. Power and Water Authority* (2004) 219 CLR 90, [124].
219. *NT Power Generation Pty Ltd v. Power and Water Authority* (2004) 219 CLR 90, [85].
220. Although clearly not impossible – see *ACCC v. Pfizer Australia Pty Ltd* [2018] FCAFC 78.
221. See, for example, *Pont Data Australia v. ASX Operations Pty Ltd* (1990) 21 FCR 385.
222. (1990) 21 FCR 385.

249. Wilcox J held that the new wholesale price charged to Pont Data did not reflect the costs incurred in providing the information[223] and that ASX Operations was in a position to impose those terms only because of its market power.[224] This new agreement was imposed on Pont Data primarily for the purpose of preventing Pont Data competing with ASX Operations' retail division, as revealed by documentary evidence to this effect.[225] Wilcox J cited the High Court's decision in *Queensland Wire Industries Pty Ltd v. Broken Hill Pty Co Ltd*[226] to reject a proposition by ASX Operations that they could simply refuse to supply Pont Data.[227] On appeal, the Full Court upheld this finding, stating that ASX Operations took advantage of its market power (or in current language, substantially lessened competition) for the purpose of deterring retail competitors from engaging in competitive conduct in imposing the new agreement on Pont Data.[228]

---

223. *ASX Operations Pty Ltd v. Pont Data Australia Pty Ltd (No. 1)* (1990) 21 FCR 385, 415.
224. *ASX Operations Pty Ltd v. Pont Data Australia Pty Ltd (No. 1)* (1990) 21 FCR 385, 417.
225. *ASX Operations Pty Ltd v. Pont Data Australia Pty Ltd (No. 1)* (1990) 21 FCR 385, 417–418.
226. (1989) 167 CLR 177.
227. *ASX Operations Pty Ltd v. Pont Data Australia Pty Ltd (No. 1)* (1990) 21 FCR 385, 419.
228. *ASX Operations Pty Ltd v. Pont Data Australia Pty Ltd* (1990) 27 FCR 460, 486. See further Stephen Corones, 'Crossing a Shadowy Barrier: Recent Price Squeeze Cases', *Australian Business Law Review* 19 (1991): 284.

Chapter 3. Concentrations

§1. The Relevant Prohibition: Section 50 CCA

250. Merger activity is important for the efficient functioning of the economy. A merger may improve the merged entity's profitability by allowing the entity to achieve efficiencies stemming from the achievement of economies of scope and scale, savings in formerly duplicated output and asset rationalization. Merger activity also ensures that the market for corporate control, in which under-performing owners or managers are replaced, functions properly. However, merger activity may also be motivated by a desire to increase profitability by strengthening market power rather than improving the efficiency of the firm's operations.

251. To ensure that the benefits brought about by mergers are not lost, only those acquisitions that would have the effect, or be likely to have the effect, of substantially lessening competition in a market[229] are prohibited.[230] The term 'substantial' is not defined in the legislation. It has been interpreted to require that the effect be 'meaningful or relevant to the competitive process'[231] or 'real or of substance'.[232] It is not necessary to establish that the effect is 'more probable than not'.[233] The word likely requires that there be a 'real chance or possibility' that competition will be substantially lessened by the merger.[234] The substantial lessening of competition need not be 'more probable than not' for an acquisition to contravene the merger prohibition.[235]

252. The merger prohibition requires a forward-looking analysis that compares likely future states. The likely 'future with' the merger is identified as is the likely 'future without' the merger. By comparing these two states, the impact of the merger on competition can be isolated.[236] In *Australian Competition and Consumer Commission v. Metcash Trading Ltd*,[237] the Full Federal Court left unresolved as to whether in considering the counterfactual (i.e., the competitive results if the future

229. The prohibition actually refers to a substantial market. It appears that the reference to a substantial market is included to exclude a merger that occurs in a very small market from the reach of the merger prohibition. The courts have not yet had to determine when a market is to be considered substantial.
230. Between 1977 and 1993, acquisitions were only prohibited if they created or enhanced a position of dominance in a market. Decisions handed down during this period should be read with this in mind.
231. *Rural Press Limited v. Australian Competition and Consumer Commission* (2003) 216 CLR 53, 71.
232. *Radio 2UE Sydney Pty Ltd v. Stereo FM Pty Ltd* (1982) 44 ALR 557, 564. See also *Tillmanns Butcheries Pty Ltd v. Australian Meat Employees' Union* (1979) 27 ALR 367.
233. *Australian Gas Light Company v. Australian Competition and Consumer Commission (No. 3)* (2003) 137 FCR 317, 415.
234. *Australian Gas Light Company v. Australian Competition and Consumer Commission (No. 3)* (2003) 137 FCR 317, 415.
235. *Monroe Topple & Associates Pty Ltd v. The Institute of Chartered Accountants (Aust)* (2002) 122 FCR 110, 140.
236. *Australian Gas Light Company v. Australian Competition and Consumer Commission* (2003) 137 FCR 317, 417.
237. (2011) 198 FCR 297.

did not include the deal) the standard of proof was that of a real chance or possibility in determining whether there was a lessening of competition, or whether it needed to be considered on the balance of probabilities. If the latter, it would seem to hamper the ACCC's efforts to regulate merger activity. The matter awaits resolution by a superior court.

253. The merger prohibition against acquisitions that substantially lessen competition applies to acquisitions by a corporation of shares in a body corporate or assets of a body corporate or natural person.[238] The prohibition also applies to acquisitions by a natural person of shares in a corporation or body corporate or assets of a corporation, body corporate or natural person.[239] The prohibition applies to direct acquisitions and indirect acquisitions. An entity will be taken to have made an indirect acquisition if its agent,[240] and possibly its subsidiary,[241] makes an acquisition. The prohibition is not limited to acquisitions of controlling interests.

I. Overseas Acquisitions

254. Overseas acquisitions by bodies corporate incorporated, or carrying on a business, in Australia will be caught by the merger prohibition if the merger substantially lessens competition in a market in Australia even if the acquired firm has no connection with Australia.[242] Acquisitions by bodies corporate not incorporated, or carrying on a business, in Australia that take place outside Australia are not caught by the merger prohibition. Thus, the merger prohibition would not capture merger activity engaged in outside Australia of two international holding companies even if both holding companies' own subsidiaries operated in Australia. However, where a body corporate acquires a controlling interest in another body corporate outside Australia and, by reason of the acquisition obtains a second controlling interest in a body corporate that carries out business in Australia, the ACT may make a declaration banning the parties from continuing to carry on business in Australia.[243] The Tribunal will make a declaration if the acquisition is likely to substantially lessen competition in a market in Australia and does not generate sufficient offsetting public benefits.

238. Section 50(1) *Competition and Consumer Act 2010.*
239. Sections 50(1), 50(2) and 150C *Competition and Consumer Act 2010.*
240. *Trade Practices Commission v. Australian Iron & Steel Pty Ltd* (1990) 22 FCR 305.
241. *Australia Meat Holdings Pty Ltd v. Trade Practices Commission* (1989) ATPR 40-932, 50,094; *Trade Practices Commission v. Gillette Company (No. 1)* (1993) 45 FCR 366, 377. Cf *Trade Practices Commission v. Australian Iron & Steel Pty Ltd* (1990) 22 FCR 305, 318.
242. Section 5(1) *Competition and Consumer Act 2010*; *Trade Practices Commission v. Australian Iron & Steel Pty Ltd* (1990) 22 FCR 305, 319–321.
243. Section 50A *Competition and Consumer Act 2010.*

II. Merger Factors

255. Australia's competition laws are more prescriptive than the equivalent laws in the US. Section 50(3) of the CCA sets out the following list of matters that must be taken into account in determining whether an acquisition is likely to substantially lessen competition in a market:

(a) the actual and potential level of import competition in the market;
(b) the height of barriers to entry to the market;
(c) the level of concentration in the market;
(d) the degree of countervailing power in the market;
(e) the likelihood that the acquisition would result in the acquirer being able to significantly and sustainably increase prices or profit margins;
(f) the extent to which substitutes are available in the market or are likely to be available in the market;
(g) the dynamic characteristics of the market, including growth, innovation and product differentiation;
(h) the likelihood that the acquisition would result in the removal from the market of a vigorous and effective competitor; and
(i) the nature and extent of vertical integration in the market.

256. The merger factors highlight the potential constraints on the merged firm and identify the structural features of the market, which affect the impact of the merger on competition. The merger factors are very broad and often overlap. The merger factors will assume different levels of importance depending on the merger under consideration. This list of merger factors is not exhaustive, and other relevant matters may be taken into account to determine whether or not a merger is likely to lessen competition in a market. Other potentially relevant matters include strategic or other behavioural considerations, the likelihood of coordinated conduct and efficiency enhancing aspects of a merger that affect the level of competition in the relevant market.

III. Notification

257. Merger parties are under no legislative obligation to notify Australia's competition regulator, the ACCC, before proceeding with an acquisition. However, the ACCC strongly encourages parties to do so where the products or services of the merger parties are either substitutes or complements, and the merged firm will have a post-merger market share of greater than 20% in the relevant markets. Presumably, the ACCC would also encourage parties to notify it where the merger will result in the combination of two firms operating at different functional levels of the market, although this is not expressly noted in the ACCC's Merger Guidelines.

258. To avoid the risk that the legality of the acquisition will be challenged in court by the ACCC or another interested party, merger parties typically seek informal clearance, formal clearance or authorization. Of these three processes, informal review is the most popular.

IV. Informal Clearance

259. The ACCC will provide merger parties with its informal view as to whether it believes a merger will substantially lessen competition in a market. Even if the ACCC decides to grant informal clearance of the merger, this does not confer immunity from legal action on the merger parties, nor does it raise an estoppel in favour of the merger parties. However, it is incredibly rare for legal action to be taken to challenge a merger that was informally cleared. Private litigants are strongly guided by the ACCC's assessment of the competitive effects of the merger and, in any event, are unable to seek injunctions to prevent the merger.[244] In order to maintain the high level of faith, the business community has in the informal clearance process; the ACCC will only challenge an acquisition it has informally cleared in extreme circumstances (such as when there has been a dramatic change in market conditions or the parties provided the ACCC with inaccurate or misleading information). The ACCC has issued guidelines that outline the processes that it will apply when it reviews merger activity and decides whether to grant informal clearance.[245]

V. Formal Merger Clearance

260. As of 1 January 2007, merger parties have the option of applying to the ACCC for authorization of mergers (see details below).

VI. Merger Authorization

261. The CCA makes provision for parties to seek formal authorization of mergers (see Merger Authorisation Guidelines, 2018). Authorization will be granted if the merger will not substantially lessen competition, or the benefit to the public will outweigh the detriment.

VII. Australian Merger 'Law'

262. The Australian courts have not dealt with many merger cases. In fact, there has only been one fully argued case since the substantial lessening of competition

244. See s. 80(1A) of the *Competition and Consumer Act 2010.*
245. Merger Review Process Guidelines 2008, available at www.accc.gov.au.

test was introduced in 1992.[246] Merger court decisions are so rare because merger parties typically resolve issues administratively under the clearance or authorization processes. These processes are preferred by merger parties because of the costs, delays and uncertainty associated with litigating mergers in the courts. As a result, the bulk of merger analysis is to be found in the determinations of the ACCC and the ACT rather than judicial decisions.

VIII. Enforceable Undertakings

263. Competition issues raised by a merger can potentially be overcome by the merger parties giving the ACCC a court-enforceable undertaking.[247] Merger parties may offer structural or behavioural undertakings. Structural undertakings are directed at structural issues in the relevant markets. For example, if the ACCC has concerns that the merged entity will have market power in a particular geographical region of Australia, the acquirer may offer the ACCC an undertaking that it will divest certain assets in the geographic region of concern. Behavioural undertakings are directed at the way the merged entity will behave in the future on an ongoing basis. The ACCC has a strong preference for structural undertakings as behavioural undertakings can be difficult to monitor and enforce and may also be inflexible and unresponsive to market changes. An example of a structural undertaking is a requirement that an entity divests itself of a part of its business, thus allowing a competitor to gain a foothold in that market. A behavioural undertaking is where an entity is required to maintain product range or service standards in the disputed area equivalent to the benchmarks that they would have in a competitive area. A specific example would be requiring service delivery benchmarks in regional Australia to be the equivalent of what is occurring in a major metropolitan area.

§2. Horizontal Mergers

264. Whether a horizontal merger will have the effect or be likely to have the effect of substantially lessening competition in a market will depend on the competitive constraints the firm will face following the merger. These constraints may be imposed by rivalry amongst current market participants, the bargaining power of customers and/or the threat of successful market entry.

---

246. *Australian Gas Light Company v. Australian Competition and Consumer Commission (No. 3)* (2003) 137 FCR 317.
247. See s. 87B *Competition and Consumer Act 2010.*

I. Defining the Market

265. The starting point for analysing the competitive effects of any merger is to identify the market or markets likely to be affected by the acquisition; this establishes the relevant field of inquiry for merger analysis. Identifying the relevant market allows market shares and market concentration figures to be calculated, the level of import competition to be assessed and the height of barriers to entry to be measured. In the seminal decision of *Re QCMA,*[248] the Trade Practices Tribunal (TPT) (the predecessor to the ACT) stated that 'a market is the field of actual or potential transactions between buyers and sellers amongst whom there can be strong substitution, at least in the long run, if given a sufficient price incentive'.[249] A market is a multi-dimensional concept. It is necessary to identify the product/service dimension, the geographic dimension and the functional dimension of the market.[250] The product and geographic dimensions should be the focus when determining the competitive effects of a horizontal merger. Both these dimensions are determined by substitution possibilities.[251] Both demand-side and supply-side substitution possibilities need to be considered.

266. All products and geographic sources of supply that are demand-side substitutes should be included in the market. Products or geographic sources of supply are demand-side substitutes if consumers would switch between them in response to an increase in price (or decrease in quality) of one of the products. To determine the products and geographical sources of supply that should be included in the market on the basis of demand-side substitution possibilities, the ACCC employs the Hypothetical Monopolist Test (HMT) as an intellectual aid. The HMT aims to identify the smallest area of product, geographic and functional space over which a hypothetical monopolist could impose a small but significant, non-transitory increase in price (SSNIP).[252] Analysis under the HMT starts with one of the products and geographic areas that will be supplied by the merged firm. If a hypothetical monopolist of this product selling in the identified geographic area could not impose an SSNIP because consumers would switch to alternative products or geographic sources of supply, the next best substitute is added. This process continues until a group of products and geographic source of supply is identified in which a hypothetical monopolist could profitably impose an SSNIP. It should be noted that a court hearing a merger case is unlikely to employ the HMT. Rather, it is likely that a court would undertake a more qualitative analysis.

267. Supply-side substitutes should also be included in the market. Product A will be a supply-side substitute for Product B if, in response to an increase in the

---

248. *Re Queensland Co-op Milling Association Ltd* (1976) 8 ALR 481.
249. *Re Queensland Co-op Milling Association Ltd* (1976) 8 ALR 481.
250. On occasion, the Tribunal has talked of a fourth dimension, the temporal dimension (see, for example, *Re Tooth & Co Ltd and Tooheys Ltd* (1979) ATPR para. 40-113). However, this dimension is rarely discussed in the case law and is best thought of as the time over which substitution possibilities play out.
251. Section 4E, *Competition and Consumer Act 2010.*
252. The Merger Guidelines define an SSNIP as a price rise of at least 5%.

price of Product B (or substitutes for Product B), a company producing Product A can switch its existing infrastructure quickly and without significant investment to supply Product B or a demand-side substitute for Product B. The same logic applies with respect to supply-side geographic sources of supply.

II. Assessing the Competitive Effects of a Horizontal Merger

268. Horizontal mergers involve the combination of firms operating at the same functional level and typically involve a firm acquiring one of its competitors. The primary competition concern raised by such mergers is that they result in there being one less competitor in the market. Such mergers may be motivated by a belief that the merged entity will be more profitable than the two entities operating individually. The increased profitability may stem from efficiency gains brought about by the merger. For example, the merged entity may be able to achieve economies of scale not available to the individual entities prior to the merger. However, the increased profitability may stem from the fact that the merger will increase the market power of the merged firm, thus giving it the ability to raise prices or lower quality.

269. The Merger Guidelines identify two theories of competitive harm that are relevant to assessing the competitive effects of horizontal mergers, unilateral effects and coordinated effects.

III. Unilateral Effects

270. Unilateral effects are brought about by a merger that increases the merged entity's unilateral market power.[253] For example, the combination of two firms, each with a market share of 20% and a limited ability to influence market outcomes, may create a merged entity with market power, especially where there are barriers to entering the market or the economies of scale the merged entity is now able to achieve create such barriers. The ACCC has also indicated that, when assessing the likelihood that the merger will have anticompetitive unilateral effects, it will also consider the significance of the merger parties to the competitive process, the extent of the competitive constraint the merger parties would exert on each other in the future without the merger and whether rivals have the incentive and ability to respond to a price increase (or quality reduction) by the merged entity.

IV. Coordinated Effects

271. By reducing the number of firms operating in the market, a horizontal merger may also have anticompetitive coordinated effects that alter the nature of

253. For an example of a merger authorization application refused because of concerns about unilateral effects, see *Bristile Holdings Ltd* (1997) ATPR (Com) para. 50-250.

interdependence between rivals.[254] The merger will have such effects if it makes it easier for firms to explicitly or implicitly coordinate their conduct in a more complete or sustainable way. Although a range of other factors (such as each firm's awareness of its rivals conduct, evenness of sales and homogeneity of products)[255] will also be relevant, by reducing the number of firms operating in the market a horizontal merger increases the risk of coordinated behaviour. Coordination is also more likely where market conditions are such that deviations from the coordinated conduct can be detected and effectively punished.

V. The Section 50(3) Merger Factors

272. The merger factors of particular relevance to the analysis of the competitive effects of a horizontal merger are discussed below.

A. Market Concentration: Merger Factor (c)

273. Market concentration refers to the number and size of competitors in the market. Market concentration is a necessary, but not a sufficient condition of both unilateral and coordinated effects. A firm must have a large market share in order to have unilateral market power. Coordinated effects are more likely the higher the level of market concentration. However, a firm with a large market share will not necessarily be able to act in an anticompetitive manner as it may nevertheless face constraints, such as the threat of market entry.

274. The ACCC begins its analysis by measuring market concentration levels, which are used as a filter in deciding which mergers should be subjected to a more detailed evaluation. The ACCC calculates the Herfindahl–Hirschman Index (HHI) as a preliminary indicator of the likelihood that the merger will raise competition concerns. The HHI is calculated by adding the sum of the squares of the post-merger market shares of the merged firm and each rival firm in the relevant market. The ACCC compares the HHI pre-merger with the HHI post-merger. This provides a measure of the change in market concentration caused by the merger. The Merger Guidelines state that horizontal mergers are less likely to raise competition concerns when the post-merger HHI is:

- less than 2,000; or
- greater than 2,000 (but the difference between the pre-merger and post-merger HHI is less than 100).

254. For an example of a merger authorization application refused because of concerns about coordinated effects, see *Wattyl (Aust) Pty Ltd, Courtaulds (Aust) Pty Ltd* (1996) ATPR (Com) para. 50-231.

255. See George Hay, 'Practices that Facilitate Co-operation', in *The Antitrust Revolution,* ed. J. Kwoka & L. White Scott (1989). For a discussion of these concepts in the Australian context, see Rhonda Smith, Arlen Duke & David K Round, 'Signalling, Collusion and s. 45 of the Trade Practices Act', *Competition and Consumer Law Journal* 17 (2009): 22–42.

275. A horizontal merger necessarily increases market concentration. However, this does not mean that competition will always be lessened as a result. For example, the combination of two small firms may create a firm that is better placed to compete effectively with the other firms in the market.

B. Barriers to Entry: Merger Factor (b)

276. Barriers to entry determine the ease with which new firms can enter the market and compete with existing market participants.[256] The term 'barrier to entry' has a wider meaning in the Australian legal context than it has in most economic circles. It has been described as 'a metaphor for economic disincentives for new entrants'.[257] Such disincentives may stem from the presence of economies of scale and scope, sunk costs, control over essential inputs, product differentiation, brand loyalty or legal and regulatory conditions.

277. Barriers to entry or expansion protect any unilateral market power present in the market or created by the merger. Thus, a horizontal merger that creates new barriers to entry or expansion, or raises existing barriers, is highly likely to raise competition concerns. Even if the merger leaves barriers to entry unchanged, they are still relevant to any assessment of the competitive effects of a merger. Other anticompetitive effects brought about by a merger will be magnified if barriers to entry to the market(s) affected by the merger are high. This is because barriers to entry insulate the merged entity and its rivals from the competitive constraints imposed by new entrants and the threat of new entry. Barriers to entry also increase the likelihood of coordinated effects resulting from tacit or explicit coordination and are less likely to be disrupted by a new entrant. In one of the few merger cases heard by the courts, the court granted an injunction prohibiting the merger of Australia's largest biscuit manufacturer from acquiring one of its competitors because the merged entity would have possessed a very large market share which would have been protected by barriers to entry including: high capital costs, intense brand loyalty, economies of scale and access to shelf space.[258]

278. Conversely, if barriers to entry are low, even participants in a highly concentrated market are likely to act in a competitive fashion. Contestable market theory posits that if barriers to entry are low, and thus there is always a risk of market entry, the merged entity will not have market power and, therefore, will not be able to act in an anticompetitive manner. The threat of market entry will ensure the market is competitive.

---

256. See also *Trade Practices Commission v. Ansett Transport Industries (Operations) Pty Ltd* (1978) 32 FLR 305, 325.
257. *Australian Gas Light Company v. Australian Competition and Consumer Commission (No. 3)* (2003) 137 FCR 317, 419.
258. *Arnotts Ltd v. Trade Practices Commission* (1990) 24 FCR 313.

C. Vertical Integration: Merger Factor (i)

279. Vertical relationships may be relevant to an assessment of the competitive effects of a horizontal merger. Vertical relationships may raise barriers to entry or expansion. The ACCC objected to the proposed merger between two paint manufacturers on the basis that the merger would strengthen the oligopolistic nature of the architectural and decorative paints market. The conclusion that the merger would substantially lessen competition was strengthened by the prevalence of vertical exclusivity relationships between paint manufacturers and paint resellers. These relationships restricted access to retail shelf space, thus erecting a barrier to entry and significantly reducing the likelihood that tacit or explicit coordination between market participants would be constrained by new entry or the threat of new entry.[259]

D. Import Competition: Merger Factor (a)

280. Actual or potential import competition may provide an effective constraint on domestic market participants such that a merger will not be likely to substantially lessen competition.[260] For example, the ACCC granted informal clearance to the two remaining Australian manufacturers of white goods because it believed they would face significant competition from imported brands.[261] In reaching the conclusion that the merger would not substantially lessen competition, the ACCC noted that a range of competitively priced imported products was available in the market that importers were able to establish adequate distribution channels and provide after-sales service.

281. The increasing internationalization of the Australian economy means that import competition is an important element in assessing the competitive effects of mergers. In its Merger Guidelines, the ACCC indicates that a merger is unlikely to substantially lessen competition where imports account for 10% of the total sales made in the previous three years, there are no barriers preventing importers from gaining further market share, they are viewed by consumers as close substitutes to the products or services provided by the merged firm and the importers are independent of the merged firm.

259. *Wattyl (Australia) Pty Limited, Courtaulds (Australia) Pty Limited* (1996) ATPR (Com) para. 50-232.
260. See Julie Brebner, 'The Relevance of Import Competition to Merger Assessment in Australia', *Competition and Consumer Law Journal* 10 (2002): 119.
261. ACCC Media Release MR 24/99 (11 Mar. 1999) (available at <www.accc.gov.au>). Note that no competition assessment was issued in relation to this merger.

E. Availability of Substitutes: Merger Factor (f)

282. Where the horizontal merger involves two entities that operate in differentiated product markets, unilateral effects are more likely if the merger parties are each other's closest competitors. As a result of the merger, each merger party's closest source of competitive constraint has been removed. For example, assuming that the product dimension of the market was defined to include all citrus fruits, a merger between two orange growers is likely to have a greater competitive impact than a merger between a lime grower and an orange grower.

F. Countervailing Power: Merger Factor (d)

283. Rivals are not the only source of constraint the merged entity will face. Where the merged entities' customers have a large degree of bargaining (or countervailing) power, a horizontal merger is less likely to substantially lessen competition. The merged entity's customers will have countervailing power when they can make a credible threat to bypass the merged entity. Such a threat will be credible when the customer could source its requirements from one or more of the merged entity's competitors, establish import operations, sponsor new entry or vertically integrate into the upstream market. Countervailing power will only constrain the merged entity if a significant proportion of the merged entity's customers are able to bypass the merged firm post-merger.

G. Dynamic Characteristics of the Market: Merger Factor (g)

284. Whether a market is growing or declining, the level of innovation present in the market can affect its competitiveness. These factors influence the likelihood that the merged entity will be constrained by new entrants (or the threat of new entry) and, in turn, that any market power created by the merger will be transitory in nature. Market entry is more likely where a market is growing, and technology employed in the market is changing.

H. Removal of a Vigorous and Effective Competitor: Merger Factor (h)

285. A merger is more likely to have anticompetitive effects where the firm acquired was a particularly vigorous or effective competitor responsible for driving significant aspects of competition. The acquisition of a small-scale but innovative market participant by a large, entrenched market participant may not significantly change market structure or significantly raise barriers to entry. However, it could cause competitive harm by removing from the market an entity whose activity was disrupting or undermining coordinated conduct in the market. The acquisition of such a firm is likely to have an effect on competition that is disproportionate to that firm's size.

286. A merger that removes a vigorous and effective competitor will have a greater anticompetitive effect in an oligopolistic market in which barriers to entry are high. Such markets are more reliant upon existing firms to generate competition.

I. Efficiencies

287. Even though efficiencies are not listed as a merger factor, they can nevertheless be taken into account. When determining whether or not a merger contravenes the merger prohibition, efficiencies can only be considered to the extent that they impact on the competitive process.[262] For example, the combination of two smaller competitors may create a more efficient entity that is better able to compete with its larger rivals. Such a merger is unlikely to be caught by the merger prohibition as it may very well improve the level of competition in a market. However, the merger may generate economies of scale and/or scope that raise barriers to entry.

288. Efficiencies are also relevant to Australian merger analysis in another way. As noted above, it is possible to apply to the ACT for authorization to make an acquisition. Authorization will be granted where the proposed acquisition would result, or be likely to result, in such a benefit to the public that the acquisition should be allowed to occur.[263] The principal element of recognized public benefits is the achievement of economic efficiency and progress.[264] Thus, a merger that substantially lessens competition may nevertheless be granted immunity under the authorization process if it generates substantial efficiencies.

§3. Vertical Mergers

I. Introduction

289. A vertical merger involves the combination of firms operating at different stages of a vertical supply chain. Such mergers take place between firms who are, or may be, in the relation of supplier and acquirer. The competition concern raised by such mergers is that they result in the linking of previously separate functions under the same ownership and control. From the outset, it must be noted that vertical mergers are far less likely to raise competition concerns than horizontal mergers. This is because vertical mergers do not involve the combination of two entities that were formally competitors. In fact, such mergers will often promote efficiency because of the integration of complementary activities and by allowing for greater coordination of the functions performed at different levels of the supply chain and the reduction of transaction costs.

262. See Arlen Duke, 'A More Efficient Use of Efficiencies in Merger Authorisation Determinations', *Australian Business Law Review* 34 (2007): 278.
263. Section 95AZH(1), *Competition and Consumer Act 2010.*
264. *Re Queensland Co-op Milling Association Ltd* (1976) 8 ALR 481.

II. Defining the Market

290. As with horizontal mergers, it is necessary to define the product and geographic dimensions of the market(s) in which the merged entity will operate. The process for doing so is set out above. In order to analyse the competitive effects of a vertical merger, close attention must be paid to the functional dimensions of the market in which the merged entity will operate. The functional dimension refers to the level of the supply chain at which the relevant competitive activity takes place.

291. It may be appropriate to analyse the competitive effects of the merger in one market that comprises the whole vertical supply chain or to analyse the effects of the merger in a series of separate markets, each with a different functional dimension. The former method is appropriate where there are strong efficiencies of vertical integration, or where competition at one functional level imposes a constraint on firms acting at another functional level. For example, in the context of an authorization application relating to the merger of two independent supermarket wholesalers, the tribunal found that the relevant market included both the retail and wholesale levels of the market. This was because competition at the retail level would constrain the ability of the merged independent supermarket wholesaler to increase the price or reduce quality.[265] However, in most instances it will be appropriate to identify and analyse the effects of the merger in separate markets, each with a different functional dimension.

III. Assessing the Competitive Effects of a Vertical Merger

292. The primary competition concern associated with such mergers is that they may allow the merged entity to foreclose sources of supply or sources of distribution or engage in other forms of anticompetitive behaviour. For example, if a clothing retailer and clothing wholesaler merge, the merged entity may refuse to stock clothes supplied by other wholesalers in its retail outlets. If the merged entity has a large share of the retail market, this may make it difficult for another clothing wholesaler to compete as it would struggle to find a source of distribution for its products. Vertical mergers may also allow the merged entity to raise rivals' costs by charging downstream competitors a high price for an essential input (or, worse still, limit or deny access to that input).

293. Vertical mergers will only substantially lessen competition in the manner outlined above, where prior to the merger one of the firms had substantial market power at one functional level of the market level and the merged entity will have the incentive to exploit that market power when it operates in a related upstream or

265. *Re QIW* (1995) ATPR para. 41-438.

downstream market.[266] For example, the merged entity will only be able to successfully engage in foreclosure strategies against a rival firm operating in the downstream market if the merged entity will have sufficient market power in the upstream market. Absent such power, the rival operating in the downstream market will be able to bypass the merged entity and secure supply from other firms operating in the upstream market. Whether or not the merged entity has market power in the upstream market will depend on the number of players operating in the upstream market, the height of barriers to entry in the upstream market, the significance of the input to the downstream rival and whether downstream rivals have countervailing power (which may result from an ability of downstream rivals to commence operations in the upstream market). Similarly, the merged firm will only be able to successfully engage in foreclosure strategies against a rival firm operating in an upstream market if it has sufficient market power in the downstream market. Returning to the example of the merged clothing wholesaler and retailer, it would not be possible for the merged entity to make it difficult for other clothing wholesalers by refusing to stock the other wholesaler's goods in the merged entity's retail stores if the retail market is competitive. Other wholesalers would still be able to distribute their goods in other retail outlets.

294. A vertical merger might allow the merged entity to gain access to sensitive information about the activities of upstream or downstream competitors. A firm operating at two functional levels of the market may supply its competitors in an upstream or downstream market. For example, a vertically integrated firm that operates in the gas production and gas distribution market will have access to sensitive information about the activities of other gas producers who are forced to obtain distribution services from the vertically integrated firm. It is once again worth noting that the potential anticompetitive effects stem from the fact that the vertically integrated firm has market power at one of the functional levels of the market at which it operates (in this example, the firm is very likely to have market power in the gas distribution market as distribution facilities often constitute natural monopolies).

295. Vertical mergers may also raise barriers to entry where the nature and extent of vertical integration or vertical relationships are already high. For example, if most manufacturers operating in a particular market also own retail outlets, or have strong vertical ties with retailers, then a vertical merger between two previously independent firms may raise barriers to the manufacturing market. This is because a new entrant to the manufacturing level may be compelled to set up retail operations in order to effectively compete because existing sources of distribution are either owned by or tied up by the entrant's competitors at the manufacturing

266. The Trade Practices Tribunal has expressed the view that it is prima facie undesirable to have vertical integration between a producer with market power and a major distributor of the product as this could harm competition in both the production and distribution markets: *Re Rural Traders Co-Op (Western Australia) Ltd* (1979) 37 FLR 244, 282.

level.[267] Whether this is an arduous requirement will depend on the height of barriers to entry to the retail market. Where the level of vertical integration between manufacturers and retailers is high, it will be important to consider whether economies of scale at the retail act as a barrier to entering the retail market and in turn, the manufacturing market.

IV. The Section 50(3) Merger Factors

296. As noted above, section 50(3) of the CCA sets out a list of matters that must be taken into account in determining whether an acquisition is likely to substantially lessen competition. Merger factor (i), which directs attention to the nature and extent of vertical integration in the market, is directly relevant to an analysis of the likely competitive effects of vertical mergers. As explained above, the merged entity will not be able to act anticompetitively unless it has substantial market power at one functional level. As a result, many of the other merger factors which determine whether or not a merged firm is likely to have market power at one or both of the functional levels at which it operates are also highly relevant. The height of barriers to entry (merger factor (b)), the level of import competition (merger factor (a)), the level of concentration in the market (merger factor (c)) and the dynamic characteristics of the market (merger factor (g)) are all highly relevant to an assessment of whether the merged entity will have market power in any of the functional markets in which it operates.

§4. Market/Product Extension Mergers

I. Introduction

297. Extension mergers allow companies to extend the base of their operations as well as the range of products and services they supply. Like vertical mergers, extension mergers do not involve the combination of former competitors and are, therefore, much less likely to raise competition concerns than horizontal mergers. Extension mergers pose no threat to competition if the merged entity lacks substantial market power in one (or more) of the markets in which it operates.

298. Extension mergers can improve efficiency and possibly increase the level of competition in the market where a firm is able to take advantage of economies of scale or scope because of commonality in operations. However, where the merged firm has market power in one (or more) markets, an extension merger may provide the merged firm with the ability and incentive to tie or bundle products in the markets in which it operates. Such conduct raises competition concerns because of the

267. For a discussion of the effects of relationships between firms operating at different functional levels on competition, albeit in the context of a horizontal merger, see *Wattyl (Aust) Pty Ltd, Courtaulds (Aust) Pty Ltd* (1996) ATPR (Com) para. 50-231.

potential that it will foreclose market opportunities that would otherwise be open to the merged firm's rivals and in turn, limit or raise the cost of rival firms' access to a sufficient customer base.

II. Market Extension Merger

299. A market extension merger involves the combination of two entities that sell the same product or service but in separate geographic markets. Imagine that the wholesale market for a particular product is divided into a series of geographic markets that are roughly defined by state borders. The combination of a wholesaler that sold to the New South Wales market with a wholesaler that serviced the Victorian market would constitute a market extension merger.

300. Market extension mergers are likely to be motivated by a desire to reap efficiency gains. A market extension merger may also be a natural and efficient way for a firm to expand its operations. For example, a merged firm may be able to operate in several geographic markets while only maintaining a single head office in one geographic region. However, market extension mergers may have anticompetitive consequences. Such mergers may allow the merged firm to tie supply in one geographic market to another geographic market. Returning to the example provided in the preceding paragraph, if the merged wholesaler had market power in the Victorian market, it may tie sales in that market to sales in the New South Wales market, in which it has no market power. This could foreclose opportunities available to the merged entity's competitors in the New South Wales market. It is important not to overstate the likelihood of such anticompetitive effects though. Such conduct would only be possible if the firm had substantial market power in the Victorian market and that market power was protected by barriers to entry. To make an assessment of market power and barriers to entry, it is necessary to consider the level of import competition (merger factor (a)), the level of concentration in the market (merger factor (c)) and the dynamic characteristics of the market (merger factor (g)), all of which have been discussed above.

301. A series of market extension mergers may, over time, enable the merged entity to achieve substantial economies of scale. While this improves the efficiency of the merged firm, it may also raise barriers to entry and may have an anticompetitive effect. A firm contemplating entering the market may be dissuaded from doing so because it recognizes that it will not be able to reach the minimum efficient scale required to be competitive in the market. Many argue that Australia's two large supermarket chains have substantial market power because they have, over time engaged in a string of market extension mergers, none of which, taken alone, resulted in a substantial lessening of competition. In response to such concerns, the Australian Government is currently considering whether Australia's merger laws need to be amended to capture such mergers, which are commonly referred to as creeping acquisitions.

III. Product Extension Merger

302. A product extension merger involves the combination of two entities that sell related products. Even though the two entities sell different products, these products may be to some extent substitutable, or they may be complementary. A product extension merger may be a natural and efficient way for a firm to expand its operations to include natural product extensions. However, such a merger may also provide the merged firm with the opportunity to bundle or tie products in an anti-competitive manner (although in order to do so, it will need market power in the market for the tying product).

303. An example of a product extension merger that raised competition issues can be found in Coca-Cola Amatil Limited's (CCA) unsuccessful attempt to acquire Berri Limited (Berri). The ACCC refused CCA's request for informal clearance to acquire fruit beverage manufacturer Berri.[268] The ACCC formed the opinion that two related, yet distinct product markets would be affected by the merger, namely the carbonated soft drinks market and the fruit beverages market and a conclusion was reached that the proposed product extension merger would have the effect, or be likely to have the effect, of substantially lessening competition in the wholesale fruit beverages market. CCA had a 67% share of the carbonated soft drinks market, largely because it distributed Coca-Cola. CCA's large market share and significant brand loyalty gave it market power in the carbonated soft-drink market. The ACCC concluded that if the merger went ahead, CCA would have the ability and incentive to leverage its market power in the carbonated soft-drinks market into the fruit beverages market by bundling its soft-drink products with Berri's fruit beverages. The contemplated bundling was likely to be effective because the complementary bundled products would be sold by the same retailers and because of Coca-Cola's status as a 'must stock' item for major retailers.

304. It is important to note the ACCC's conclusion that the merger would be anticompetitive is intrinsically linked to CCA's substantial market power in the carbonated soft drinks market. If the merged entity lacked this power, it would not have been able to coerce its customers to acquire the Berri fruit beverage products. In fact, bundling its soft-drink and fruit beverage products may simply have made its product offering uncompetitive relative to that offered by its competitors. This emphasizes the point that when analysing the competitive effects of extension mergers, one should start by asking whether the merged entity would possess substantial market power in any of the markets in which it is likely to operate. As any market power created by the merger will be temporary unless it is protected by barriers to entry, it will also be necessary to consider, amongst other things, the height of barriers to entry (merger factor (b)), the level of import competition (merger factor (a)), the level of concentration in the market (merger factor (c)) and the dynamic characteristics of the market (merger factor (g)).

---

268. *Coca-Cola/Berri* Public Competition Assessment (8 Oct. 2003) (available at <www.accc.gov.au>).

§5. Pure Conglomerate Mergers

305. A pure conglomerate merger involves the combination of two entities that do operate in the same market, do not sell products that are related to each other and do not have a supplier-customer relationship. A firm may undertake a conglomerate merger to diversify its operations and reduce risk.

306. Although a firm could diversify by starting up a new company that sells unrelated products, it is usually faster to purchase a growing concern than it is to build from the beginning. Where executive salaries are tied to revenue, a strong incentive to grow is created. This may motivate a conglomerate merger where horizontal, vertical or extension mergers are not commercially viable. This desire to grow may see firms seeking out pure conglomerate mergers even though such mergers are unlikely to generate substantial efficiencies because of the disparity of operations between the firms combined.

307. As with extension mergers, conglomerate mergers are only likely to pose a threat to competition if the merged entity has market power in one (or more) of the markets in which it operates. The concern is that the merged entity will be able to leverage that market power into the unrelated markets in which it operates by tying products over which it has market power with products in the other unrelated market. This, in turn, forecloses market opportunities that would otherwise be open to the merged firm's rivals and, in turn, limits or raises the cost of rival firms' access to a sufficient customer base.

308. Pure conglomerate mergers are less likely to pose a threat to competition than extension mergers. As a result of a pure conglomerate merger, the merged entity will operate in two unrelated markets. It is more difficult to tie or bundle products sold in completely unrelated markets because the merged entity's customers simply may not be interested in purchasing products from both markets. Returning to the CCA example above, it is likely that prior to the merger, many of CCA's customers were also customers of Berri or one of Berri's competitors. This increased the likelihood that bundling or tying by the merged entity would be effective. Imagine now that a hardware wholesaler and a fruit wholesaler combined as the result of a pure conglomerate merger. Hardware retailers simply have no need for the products offered by the fruit wholesaler. Similarly, fruit retailers (who would include supermarkets) have a very minimal need for hardware products. Thus, the merged entity in this hypothetical example would be less likely to engage in bundling or tying. Rather, any market power it possessed in the fruit or hardware wholesaling markets would most likely be exploited solely through the charging of higher prices. This is not to say that customers of firm formed as the result of a conglomerate merger will never require the products sold by the two formerly independent entities. However, the likelihood that this will be the case is less and, in turn, so is the likelihood that the merged entity can engage in effective bundling and tying strategies that pose a threat to competition.

Part III. Administrative Procedure

Chapter 1. Administrative Investigations Before the Antitrust Authority

§1. INITIATIVE

I. General Sectors Inquiries

309. The ACCC may consider enforcement proceedings in a number of ways. It may start a general inquiry into the business activities of a particular company or an individual, or it may decide to review an entire sector.

310. The ACCC also publishes regulatory reports for the seven major airports (Sydney, Melbourne, Brisbane, Perth, Adelaide, Canberra and Darwin). It is also responsible for:

- enforcing water charge and market rules;
- monitoring access to interstate rail tracks and monitoring freight prices;
- administering international liner cargo shipping arrangements and assesses stevedoring prices in the ports of Sydney, Melbourne, Brisbane, Fremantle, Adelaide and Burnie;
- monitoring charges for postal services;
- monitoring bank fees and charges in the banking sector; and
- monitoring medical indemnity premiums in the insurance sector.

II. Ex Officio Investigations

311. The ACCC has the power pursuant to section 28 of the CCA to conduct research in relation to matters affecting the interests of consumers, being matters with respect to which Parliament has the power to make laws.

III. Complaints

312. The ACCC may investigate allegations of breaches of the CCA when possible breaches are brought to the ACCC's attention by:

- complaints received from members of the public (or from business), whether they be consumers, suppliers or competitors;
- businesses and/or individuals informing the ACCC themselves if they have been directly or indirectly involved in a possible breach or seen a possible breach happen;
- the media;
- the ACCC's own staff; and
- other agencies (such as an Industry Ombudsman) or state or territory fair trading authorities.

The ACCC's power to investigate breaches is drawn from a wide range of provisions within the CCA.

313. The ACCC cannot pursue all complaints it receives, and enforcement priority will depend on a wide range of factors. Considerations that have been relevant in the past include whether the matter is of significant public interest or concern; whether there is significant detriment; does the conduct involve a blatant disregard of the law; is the matter concerning a national focus; has the behaviour targeted a vulnerable group; is the issue relating to a new market; does it involve industry wide conduct; would intervention have a strong educative effect; and finally, whether there is any sense of recidivism on the part of the contravening party or industry. Where the ACCC does not pursue a complaint, it may refer the complaint to another agency or the state or territory fair trading authorities for further investigation and resolution, or it may suggest parties consider pursuing the matter privately. Should the ACCC decide not to investigate and refer the matter to another agency, the complainant will generally be informed of this. Advice of this need not be formal.

§2. Powers

I. Request for Information

314. When the ACCC commences an investigation, it may contact potential witnesses and/or defendants and make an informal request of information, or it may do so formally (section 155).

315. The ACCC does not do private deals, and every enforcement matter that is dealt with through litigation or formal resolution is made public. However, in general, investigations are conducted confidentially, and the ACCC does not comment on matters it may or may not be investigating.

II. Investigating and Search Powers

316. The ACCC has been given a number of investigation powers under the CCA. Under section 155(1)(a), the ACCC can issue a notice, requiring a person to furnish information, produce documents or appear before the ACCC where the

ACCC (or its Chairperson or Deputy Chairperson) has 'reason to believe' that the person is capable of furnishing information, producing documents or giving evidence relating to a matter that constitutes (or may constitute) a contravention of the CCA. It is an offence to fail to comply with the notice or to furnish information or give evidence that is false or misleading. In addition, a person is not excused from furnishing information or documents on the ground that the information or document may tend to incriminate that person, although there are limitations on the admissibility in evidence against the person of such information or document in criminal proceedings. Under section 155(1)(b), the ACCC has similar powers to demand the production of documents. Under section 155(1)(c), the ACCC can issue a notice requiring a person 'to appear before the Commission at a time and place specified in the notice to give any such evidence, either orally or in writing, and produce any such documents'. A person appearing before the ACCC in response to such a notice is treated in the same way, in respect of protection and liability in any civil or criminal proceedings, as a witness in proceedings in the High Court (section 158(3)).

317. The power conferred on the ACCC by section 155A is limited to persons in New Zealand. It entitles the ACCC where it (or the Chairperson or the Deputy Chairperson) has 'reason to believe' that a person is capable of furnishing information or producing documents relating to such a matter, to serve a written notice to furnish the information or produce the documents. It is sufficient compliance if the person produces the documents or information to the New Zealand Commerce Commission (the New Zealand Antitrust Authority). Similarly, where the Commerce Commission requires a person in Australia to produce documents or furnish information, it is sufficient compliance for the person to do so to the ACCC (section 155B(1)). The ACCC is to transmit the documents or information to the Commerce Commission as soon as practicable thereafter (section 155B(2)).

318. Part XID of the CCA provides the ACCC with the power to enter premises, either with the consent of the occupier or under a search warrant issued by a magistrate. Entry onto premises with the consent of the occupier requires the ACCC to have reasonable grounds for suspecting that there may be relevant material on the premises: section 154D. On entry, the ACCC may search the premises and make hard or electronic copies of the material or secure that material: section 154E. It may remove copies but may only remove originals with the consent of the occupier.

319. If entry is pursuant to an enforceable search warrant, the ACCC office has the power to:

- enter the premises (using such force against persons and things as is necessary and reasonable in the circumstances: section 154L, but generally giving any persons at the premises an opportunity to allow entry: section 154M);
- search the premises for the material specified in the warrant;
- seize that material, if it believes it is necessary to prevent the concealment, loss or destruction of the material;
- make copies of that material;

- operate electronic equipment at the premises, such as computers, to see if the kind of material specified in the warrant is accessible by doing so;
- take equipment and material onto the premises to do these things: (section 154G).

The ACCC officer must make a copy of the search warrant available to the occupier of the premises if the occupier is present at the time the search warrant is being executed: (section 154N).

320. The search warrant must set out:

- a description of the premises to which the warrant relates, including the address;
- the kind of evidential material that is to be searched for under the warrant;
- the contraventions of the Competition and Consumer Act to which the warrant relates;
- the name of the inspector who is to be responsible for executing the warrant;
- the times at which the warrant may be executed. It may be executable at any time of the day or night, or during specified hours of the day or night; and
- the day (not more than one week after the issue of the warrant) on which the warrant ceases to have effect: (section 154X).

321. The ACCC will usually seek to examine such things as files, reports and emails and seize computer hard drives. The occupier of the premises is entitled to observe the search being conducted. However, the occupier must not obstruct an ACCC officer during the search, as the occupier can lose the right to observe the search in those circumstances: section 154P. The occupier must provide reasonable facilities and assistance to the ACCC during the search: section 154Q. This generally includes:

- opening locked doors, drawers and cabinets;
- if asked where particular documents are, informing the investigators of the location of the documents;
- not hiding or destroying documents; and
- if asked for information or things required to facilitate the investigation, such as a computer password, a key for a locked door, drawer or cabinet or the location of certain files, they should be given.

322. The occupier must answer questions or produce evidential material that relates to the warrant, on request: section 154R, or may incur a penalty for failing to do so. Failure to comply with this results in an offence, with a maximum penalty of thirty penalty units (one unit is the equivalent of a monetary sum). The obligation to answer questions does not extend to matters that have nothing to do with the ACCC's search. For example, questions relating to the contravention under investigation are not questions relating to the search. The ACCC is obliged to provide a receipt for things seized under warrant: section 154T. Two or more things may be covered in one receipt. The things must be returned within sixty days unless the

ACCC has a court order extending the retention period: section 154U. The ACCC cannot compel a person to produce a document that would disclose information that is subject to legal professional privilege.

III. Cooperation with Other State Institutions

323. The ACCC has cooperation agreements with each of the state and territory fair trading agencies. It has also signed a Memorandum of Understanding with the CDPP in relation to criminal investigations of cartel conduct. The ACCC also has agreements with other government agencies (such as the Australian Securities and Investments Commission (ASIC), the Australian Prudential Regulation Authority, the Telecommunications Industry Ombudsman).

§3. Right of Defence

I. Content and Notification of Opening Decisions

324. In Australia, the ACCC will need to bring formal court proceedings (or seek an undertaking from an entity) following an investigation. Therefore, this discussion will outline the procedure on the presumption that court proceedings have been instituted – the system in Australia is not inquisitorial. In doing this, the ACCC will issue some type of writ and statement or claim to outlining the allegations. In response to this, the defendant will reply with a defence where they may deny the material facts, admit those facts or allege that while the facts are true, they do not give rise to any legal cause of action.

II. The Proceedings: Hearings, Access to File, Briefs

325. There are many pre-trial manoeuvres in Australia. Key aspects include the right of discovery whereby each party is able to access documents in possession of the other party that may be relevant to the dispute. Depending on the Rules of Court, interrogatories can also be issued. These are questions on factual matters that are required to be answered, on oath, by the parties. These interrogatories are designed to elucidate the areas of dispute before the trial begins.

III. Statement of Objections

326. As part of normal civil procedure, defendants are able to file a defence that formally answers the points made by the plaintiff in the writ and statement of claim.

IV. Final Hearing and Decision

327. Given the adversarial nature of litigation in Australia, the Court will review the written material, and then hear the evidence from both sides during a trial before making a final decision.

Chapter 2. Voluntary Notifications and Clearance Decisions Merger Control

§1. Preliminary Filing Obligations

I. Criteria and Thresholds

328. Merger parties are under no legislative obligation to notify Australia's competition regulator, the ACCC, before proceeding with an acquisition. However, the ACCC strongly encourages parties to do so where the products or services of the merger parties are either substitutes or complements, and the merged firm will have a post-merger market share of greater than 20% in the relevant markets. Where merger parties are uncertain about how to define the relevant market, market shares should be based on the narrowest potential market definition. Presumably, the ACCC also encourages parties to notify it where the merger will result in the combination of two firms operating at different functional levels of the market and the merged firm will have a market share of greater than 20% at one functional level, although this is not expressly stated in the ACCC's merger guidelines (discussed below).

329. The ACCC has issued guidelines that outline its approach to assessing the competitive effects of mergers (Merger Guidelines).[269] The Merger Guidelines have no statutory effect and have never been referred to by a court hearing a merger matter. However, they provide a useful insight into the approach adopted by the ACCC when it assesses mergers. As the majority of merger determinations are made outside the court system, the Merger Guidelines remain very influential in practice.

II. Turnover Calculation

330. Based on the approach outlined in the Merger Guidelines, the ACCC does not use turnover to filter mergers that potentially raise a competition concern from those that do not.

III. Market Share Calculation

331. The ACCC uses market share data in two ways. First, as noted above, the ACCC encourages merger parties to notify it of the merger where the products or services of the merger parties are either substitutes or complements, and the merged firm will have a post-merger market share of greater than 20% in the relevant markets. Second, the ACCC uses market share data to calculate the HHI as a preliminary indicator of the likelihood that the merger will raise competition concerns. The HHI is calculated by adding the sum of the squares of the post-merger market shares

269. Merger Guidelines (November 2008), available at <www.accc.gov.au>.

of the merged firm and each rival firm in the relevant market. Imports and supply-side substitutes should be included in these calculations.

332. The Merger Guidelines state that the ACCC will generally calculate market shares according to sales, volume and capacity. No indication is given as to how the ACCC selects which of these measures to use, although experience suggests that the ACCC will choose the measure that best captures the competitive dynamics of the market(s) affected by the merger. The ACCC compares the HHI pre-merger with the HHI post-merger. This provides a measure of the change in market concentration caused by the merger. The Merger Guidelines state that horizontal mergers are less likely to raise competition concerns when the post-merger HHI is:

- less than 2,000; or
- greater than 2,000 (but the difference between the pre-merger and post-merger HHI is less than 100).

333. However, even within these limits, there may be other factors that suggest that the merger will have anticompetitive effects. The ACCC will, therefore, consider all of the relevant section 50(3) merger factors (see section 9).

IV. Other Relevant Notions

334. Although parties have the option of proceeding with the merger without seeking any regulatory consideration, merger parties typically seek to obtain some assurance that the merger will not be challenged by seeking informal clearance, formal clearance or authorization. These processes are explained in section 9.

§2. Structure of Proceedings

I. Preliminary Assessment and Full Investigation

335. The ACCC investigates mergers that potentially raise competition concerns. The ACCC conducts confidential and public reviews of mergers, although it is often reluctant to provide an unqualified view until the matter becomes public, and it has been able to undertake market enquiries. In addition to the guidelines issued in November 2008 that outline the approach the ACCC will adopt when assessing the competitive effects of a merger,[270] the ACCC has issued guidelines that outline the processes that it will follow in making this assessment.[271] It has also issued guidelines that outline the processes that it will follow when assessing formal clearance applications.[272]

270. Merger Guidelines (November 2008), available at <www.accc.gov.au>.
271. Merger Review Process Guidelines (June 2008), available at <www.accc.gov.au>.
272. Formal Merger Review Process Guidelines (June 2008), available at <www.accc.gov.au>.

II. Time Framework

A. *Informal Clearance*

336. When undertaking an informal clearance, the ACCC will publish an indicative timeline that will outline key dates in the process, the timing of market enquiries, dates on which submissions are due and an estimate of when the ACCC will reach a decision. Where no substantial competition concerns are raised, the review is likely to take between six and eight weeks. Where competition concerns are raised, the ACCC will issue a statement of issues (which outlines the ACCC's preliminary view), invite further submissions and undertake further market enquiries. Where this occurs, the review process is likely to take approximately twelve weeks. However, the time it takes the ACCC to process a request for informal clearance will depend on the level of information provided by the parties, the extent to which the parties cooperate and the complexity of the merger in question.

337. When the ACCC investigates mergers that it becomes aware of through channels other than direct contact from merger parties, it will follow a similar process to that adopted when processing a request for informal clearance. Where merger parties resist or delay providing the ACCC with information about the merger, this will almost certainly delay the period of time it takes the ACCC to assess the merger.

§3. Clearance and Conditional Clearance

I. Conditions and Undertakings

A. *Content*

338. The ACCC can grant authorization on certain conditions that are designed to reduce or eliminate competition concerns. Non-compliance may result in revocation of the clearance and consequent exposure to legal action under the merger prohibition.

B. *Timing*

339. Parties can offer the ACCC undertakings at any time during the merger investigation process. Where parties are aware of competition concerns raised by the proposed merger, they should consider offering undertakings as early as possible as this will ensure that the assessment of the merger is not delayed unnecessarily by the need to negotiate such undertakings and undertake additional market enquiries in relation to the undertakings.

§4. Relations with Other Merger Control Authorities

I. Other Authorities within the Local Jurisdiction

A. *Foreign Investment Review Board*

340. The Foreign Investment Review Board (FIRB) examines proposals by foreign interests to undertake direct investment in Australia and makes recommendations to the Australian Government in relation to its foreign investment policy. FIRB's function is advisory only.

341. Some exceptions apply to the obligation to notify FIRB of these acquisitions.[273] Where a party advises FIRB of a proposed acquisition, FIRB will alert the ACCC to any proposed acquisitions that may raise competition concerns. Where appropriate, the ACCC and the FIRB will share information about proposed acquisitions.

B. *Australian Prudential Regulatory Authority*

342. The Australian Prudential Regulatory Authority (APRA) has responsibilities relating to acquisitions of companies and assets within the financial system.[274] The ACCC and APRA have entered into a Memorandum of Understanding (MoU), which sets out an agreed basis for policy coordination and information sharing between the ACCC and APRA.[275] Under this MoU, the ACCC and APRA agree that they will consult each other when either organization is considering a proposal for an acquisition of assets or companies involving regulated financial institutions. The ACCC and APRA also agree to share information relevant to competition in the financial system and to consult each other about relevant transactions where doing so is appropriate and consistent with their respective confidentiality and secrecy obligations. The ACCC retains the power to investigate breaches of the competition law provisions (see Part II and Part VI of the CCA).

II. International Coordination

343. Many mergers assessed by the ACCC are international in nature. The extent to which Australia's competition laws capture overseas merger activity is discussed above. The ACCC regularly shares non-confidential information with other regulators. The sharing of such information is consistent with the ICN guiding principles

273. See <www.firb.gov.au/content/Exemptions/exemptions.asp>.
274. See *Financial Sector (Transfer of Business) Act* 1999, *Life Insurance Act* 1995.
275. See <www.apra.gov.au/Media-Releases/upload/MoU-ACCC-Australian-Competition-and-Consumer-Commission.pdf>.

for coordination between regulators on mergers review.[276] Merger parties are often asked to provide a confidentiality waiver from merger parties to enable cooperation between international agencies so that the assessment of merger activity is conducted as quickly as possible. Sharing of such information in these circumstances is also consistent with the ICN's guiding principles.

344. The ACCC and the New Zealand Commerce Commission have reached a cooperation protocol designed to assist cooperation in merger review between the two agencies.[277]

276. ICN, *Guiding Principles for Merger Notification and Review*, principle 6: coordination, <www.internationalcompetitionnetwork.org/guidingprinciples.html>.
277. Available at <www.accc.gov.au>.

Chapter 3. Challenging the Administrative Decision

§1. Competent Courts

345. Exclusive jurisdiction is vested in the FCA to hear matters relating to Part IV of the CCA,[278] though on rare occasions, it is theoretically possible for courts of states and territories to have competition law matters heard before them.[279]

§2. Time Limits

346. The Federal Court Rules (Order 52, Rule 15) provides that an appeal from a decision within the Federal Court system must be filed and served within twenty-eight days of the original decision.

§3. Scope of Judicial Review

347. Judicial Review is possible of decisions of the ACCC,[280] or the ACT. Normal appeal processes would apply to decisions of the Federal Court. Reviews of the decisions of the regulator in respect of authorization applications are reviewable by the ACT.[281] The review is a full re-hearing of the matter.[282]

278. Section 86, *Competition and Consumer Act 2010.*
279. *Jurisdiction of Courts (Cross-vesting)Act* 1987, s. 3.
280. See *Administrative Decisions (Judicial Review) Act 1977.*
281. Section 101, *Competition and Consumer Act 2010.*
282. *Re Application by Medicines Australia Inc* [2007] ACompT 4.

Selected Bibliography

Articles and Books

Ahdar, R. 'The Unfulfilled Promise of New Zealand's Monopolisation Law: Sources, Symptoms and Solutions'. *Competition and Consumer Law Journal* 16, no. 3 (2009): 291.

Andrews, S. 'Section 87B Undertakings: Practice, Principles and Pitfalls'. *Trade Practices Law Journal* 18 (2010): 244.

Australian Government. *Competition Policy Review: Final Report* (March, 2015) (known as the Harper Report).

Baird, J. & W. Robertson. 'Competition and Intellectual Property: The Intersection of Competition and Intellectual Property Law and the "New Economy"'. *Competition and Consumer Law Journal* 16 (2008): 143.

Beaton-Wells, C. 'Mergers without Markets? Unilateral Effects Analysis In the United States and Its Prospects In Australia'. *Australian Business Law Review* 34 (2006): 186.

Bezzi, M. 'The Conduct of Cartel Litigation: The ACCC Enforcement Perspective on Serious Cartels: Some Key Issues and Practical Considerations'. *Australian and New Zealand Trade Practices La Bulletin* 24 (2009): 109.

Blycha, N. & J. Duns. 'Tying, Bundling, Loyalty Rebates and Exclusive Dealing In US Antitrust: What Australia Can Learn'. *Trade Practices Law Journal* 14 (2006): 26.

Bull, M & D. Wood. 'Holding Out for a Hero: Assessing Mergers between Potential Competitors', (2012) 20 *CCLJ* 125.

Christopher, A. & S. Andrews 'Gender Disparity in Cartel Conduct' *Australian Business Law Review* 46 (2018) 237

Christopher, A & T. Fabricius, 'In Competition with Each Other? Implications of the apparently divergent outcomes in Flight Centre and ANZ', *Australian Journal of Competition and Consumer Law* 23 (2015): 6.

Clarke, J. 'Section 46: Its Purpose and the Proposed New Effects Test' *Australian Business Law Review* 45 (2017): 364.

Clarry, D. 'Contemporary Approaches to Market Definition: Taking Account of International Markets In Australian Competition Law'. *Australian Business Law Review* 37 (2009): 143.

Clough, D. 'Co-existence of Fairness and Competition under the Competition and Consumer Act 2010'. *Australian Business Law Review* 33 (2005): 99.

Selected Bibliography

Corones, S. 'Market Definition In the Age of the Internet'. *Australian Business Law Review* 38 (2010): 309.

Corrigan, M. 'Passing the Hat Around? Contribution Claims amongst Cartel Members'. *Competition and Consumer Law Journal* 16 (2009): 346.

Duke, A. 'A More Efficient Use of Efficiencies In Merger Authorisation Determinations'. *Australian Business Law Review* 35 (2007): 278.

Fisse, B. 'The First Cartel Offence Prosecution in Australia: Implications and Non-Implications' (2017) *Australian Business Law Review* 45 (2017): 482

Foster, L., & K. Hanna 'Concerted Practices: A contravention without a definition' *Competition and Consumer Law Journal* 26 (2018) 1

Gans, J. 'Protecting Consumers by Protecting Competition: Does Behavioural Economics Support this Contention?'. *Competition and Consumer Law Journal* 13 (2005): 40.

Griggs, L. & E. Sharp. 'The Homogeneity of Object in Part IV – Consumer Sovereignty as the Answer?'. *Competition and Consumer Law Journal* 11 (2003): 141.

Healey, E. & R Smith. 'Competitive Neutrality in Australia: opportunity for policy development' *Competition and Consumer Law Journal* 25 (2018) 223

Hodgeskiss, C. 'Cartels and the Competition and Consumer Act 2010 (Cth)' *Commercial Law Quarterly* 27 (2013) 8.

Holden, R. 'Competitive Neutrality in industry equilibrium' *Competition and Consumer Law Journal* 25 (2018): 267

Kemp, K. "Misuse of Market Power in Australia and Abuse of Dominance in Canada: Two legislated effects tests for unilateral conduct' *Australian Journal of Competition and Consumer Law* 26 (2018) 174.

King, S. 'The Use of Empirical Methods In Merger Investigations'. *Australian Business Law Review* 34 (2006): 227.

Lee, T. & S. Hank. 'Abuser Pays: Compensating the Victims of Cartel Conduct'. *Trade Practices Law Journal* 16 (2008): 285.

Leuner, T. 'Time and the Dimensions of Substantiality'. *Australian Business Law Review* 36 (2008): 327.

Morawetz, B. 'Identifying and Evaluating Mavericks in Australian and US Merger Analysis', *ABLR* 42 (2014): 292.

Morgan, B. & S. Bai; J Bhasker. 'Competitive Neutrality and the challenge of social enterprise' *Competition and Consumer Law Journal* 25 (2018): 249.

Mortensen, J. 'When it's Good to Be a Failure ... a Consideration of the ACCC's Recent Acceptance for the Failing Firm Counterfactual'. *Trade Practices Law Journal* 17 (2009): 151.

Nicholls, R. 'Making the Dual Model Work: competitive neutrality and net neutrality issues facing the Australian Broadcasting Commission' *Competition and Consumer Law Journal* 25 (2018) 301

Nicholls, R. & B. Fisse, 'Concerted Practices and algorithmic coordination: Does the new Australian law compute' 26 (2018) 82

Quo, S. 'Competition, Monopoly and the Role of Intent in s 2 of the Sherman Act: Lessons from Abroad'. *Australian Business Law Review* 38 (2010): 270.

Smith, R., A. Duke & D. Round. 'Signalling, Collusion and s 45 of the Trade Practices Act'. *Competition and Consumer Law Journal* 17 (2009): 22–42.

Smith, R. & R. David. 'Section 46: A Strategic Analysis of *Boral*'. *Australian Business Law Review* 30 (2002): 202.

Smith, R. & R. Trindade. 'Modernising Australian Merger Analysis'. *Australian Business Law Review* 35 (2007): 358.

Stewart, I. 'Contrary to Fact: Competition, Market Power, and the Use and Abuse of the Counterfactual Test in s 46' *ABLR* 43 (2015): 6.

Stewart, I. 'Extraterritorial Application of Part IV of the Competition and Consumer Act'. *ABLR* 42 (2014): 90.

Sweeney, B. 'International Competition Law and Policy: A Work In Progress'. *Melbourne Journal of International Law* 10 (2009): 58.

Truong, C. 'The ACCC's Immunity Policy: A New Application of the Prisoner's Dilemma'. *Trade Practices Law Journal* 15 (2007): 219.

Truong, C. 'Transnational Commerce and the Prohibition of Market Definition'. *Trade Practices Law Journal* 18 (2010): 254.

Willett, E & D. Cope. 'A new competitive neutrality' *Competition and Consumer Law Journal* 25 (2018): 280

Wylie, I. 'When Too Much Power Is Barely Enough: s 155 of the Competition and Consumer Act and Noblesse Oblige'. *Competition and Consumer Law Journal* 16 (2009): 314.

Journals

Australian Business Law Review.
Australian Journal of Competition and Consumer Law
Company and Securities Law Journal.
Competition and Consumer Law Journal.
Journal of Banking Law and Finance.
Melbourne University Law Journal.
Sydney Law Review.
University of New South Wales Law Journal.

Websites

Australian Competition and Consumer Commission <www.accc.gov.au>.
Australian Competition Law </www.australiancompetitionlaw.org/>.
Australian Legal Information Institute <www.austlii.edu.au>.
Commonwealth Legislation <www.comlaw.gov.au>.

Selected Bibliography

Table of Cases

Abott Australia [1992] ATPR (Com) 50-123.

Air New Zealand v Australian Competition and Consumer Commission; PT Garuda Indonesia Ltd v Australian Competition and Consumer Commission (2017) 91 ALJR 648

Apco Service Stations Pty Ltd v. Australian Competition and Consumer Commission [2005] ATPR 42-078.

Arnotts Ltd v. Trade Practices Commission (1990) 24 FCR 313.

Association of Fluorocarbon Consumers and Manufacturers [1994] ATPR (Com) 50-153.

ASX Operations v. Pont Data Australia Pty Ltd (No. 1) (1990) 27 FCR 460.

ASX Operations v. Pont Data Australia Pty Ltd (No. 2) (1991) 27 FCR 492.

Australia Meat Holdings Pty Ltd v. Trade Practices Commission (1989) ATPR 40-923, 50,091.

Australian Tyre Dealers' and Retreaders' Association [1994] ATPR (Com) 50-162.

ACCC v. Baxter Healthcare Pty ltd & Others (No. 2) (2008) 170 FCR 16.

ACCC v. Boral Ltd [1999] 166 ALR 410.

ACCC v. Dermalogica Pty Ltd (2005) 215 ALR 482.

ACCC v. Fila Sports Oceania Pty Ltd [2004] ATPR 41-983.

APM Investments Pty Ltd v. Trade Practices Commission (1983) 49 ALR 475.

Arcadi v. Colonial Mutual Life Assurance Society Ltd (1984) ATPR 40-473.

Australian Competition and Consumer Commission v. April International Marketing Services Australia Pty Ltd (No. 8) (2011) 277 ALR 446.

Australian Competition and Consumer Commission v. Anglo Estates Pty Ltd (2005) ATPR 42-044.

Australian Competition and Consumer Commission v Australian Competition Tribunal and Others (2017) 354 FCR 341

Australian Competition and Consumer Commission v. Australian Medical Assn Western Australia Branch Inc (2003) 199 ALR 423.

Australian Competition and Consumer Commission v. Australia and New Zealand Bank Ltd [2015] FCAFC 103.

Australian Competition and Consumer Commission v. Australian Safeway Stores Pty Ltd (2003) 129 FCR 339.

Australian Competition and Consumer Commission v. Australian Safeway Stores Pty Ltd (No. 3) [2003] FCAFC 163.

Australian Competition and Consumer Commission v. Baxter (2007) 232 CLR 1.

Australian Competition and Consumer Commission v. Baxter Healthcare (No. 2) (2008) 170 FCR 16.
Australian Competition and Consumer Commission v. Cathay Pacific Airways Ltd (No. 3) [2012] FCA 1392.
Australian Competition and Consumer Commission v. Cement Australia (2013) 310 ALR 165.
Australian Competition and Consumer Commission v Cement Australia Pty Ltd and Others (2016) 242 FCR 389
Australian Competition and Consumer Commission v. Emirates [2012] FCA 1108.
Australian Competition and Consumer Commission v. Eternal Beauty Products Pty Ltd [2012] FCA 1124.
Australian Competition and Consumer Commission v Flight Centre Travel Group Ltd (2016) 261 CLR 203
Australian Competition and Consumer Commission v. Leahy Petroleum Pty Ltd (2004) ATPR (Digest) 46-260; [2005] ATPR 42-078.
Australian Competition and Consumer Commission v. Leahy Petroleum Pty Ltd [2007] FCA 794.
Australian Competition and Consumer Commission v. Leahy Petroleum (No. 2) (2005) 215 ALR 218.
Australian Competition and Consumer Commission v. Malaysia Airline System Berhad (No. 2) [2012] FCA 767.
Australian Competition and Consumer Commission v. Metcash Trading Ltd (2011) 198 FCR 297.
Australian Competition and Consumer Commission (ACCC) v. Mitsubishi Electric Australia Pty Ltd [2013] FCA 1413.
Australian Competition and Consumer Commission v. NW Frozen Foods Pty Ltd (1996) 71 FCR 285.
Australian Competition and Consumer Commission v Oakmoore Pty Ltd [2018] FCA 1472.
Australian Competition and Consumer Commission v. Pfizer Australian Pty Ltd (2015) 110 IPR 324.
Australian Competition & Consumer Commission v. Renegade Gas Pty Ltd (trading as Supagas NSW) [2014] FCA 1135.
Australian Competition and Consumer Commission v. SIP Australia Pty Ltd (1999) ATPR paragraphs 41-702.
Australian Competition and Consumer Commission v. Thai Airways International Public Co Ltd [2012] FCA 1434.
Australian Competition and Consumer Commission v. Universal Music Australia Pty Ltd (2003) 131 FCR 529.
Australian Gas Light Co v. Australian Competition and Consumer Commission (No. 3) (2003) 137 FCR 317.
Australasian Meat Industry Employees Union & Ors v. Mudginberri Station Pty Ltd (1986) ATPR 40-709.
Boral Resources (Vic) Pty Ltd v. Construction, Forestry, Mining and Energy Union [2014] VSC 429.
Bray v. Hoffman-La Roche Ltd (2002) 118 FCR 1.
Briginshaw v. Briginshaw (1938) 60 CLR 336.

Bristile Holdings Ltd (1997) ATPR (Com) paragraphs 50-250.
Boral Besser Masonry Ltd v. Australian Competition and Consumer Commission (2003) 215 CLR 374.
Castlemaine Tooheys Ltd v. William and Hodgson Transport Pty Ltd (1986) 162 CLR 395.
Cretazzo v. Lombardi (1975) 13 SASR 4.
Dandy Power Equipment Pty Ltd v. Mercury Marine Pty Ltd (1982) 44 ALR 173.
Director of Public Prosecutions (Cth) v Nippon Yusen Kabushkik Kaisha (2017) 254 FCR 235
Eastern Express Pty Ltd v. General Newspapers Pty Ltd (1991) 30 FCR 385.
Eastern Express Pty Ltd v. General Newspapers Pty Ltd (1992) 35 FCR 43.
Epitoma Pty Ltd v. Australasian Meat Industry Employees' Union (1984) 3 FCR 55.
Flight Centre Ltd v. Australian Competition and Consumer Commission [2015] FCAFC 104.
Forster v. Farquhar (1893) 1 QB 564.
General Newspapers Pty Ltd v. Telstra Corporation (1993) 45 FCR 164.
Kadhudayan v. WD & HO Wills (Australia) Limited [2001] ATPR 41-822.
Mark Lyons Pty Ltd v. Bursill Sportsgear Pty Ltd (1987) 75 ALR 581.
Maclean v. Shell Chemical (Australia) Pty Ltd (1984) 2 FCR 593.
Melway Publishing v. Robert Hicks Pty Ltd (2001) 205 CLR 1.
Monroe Topple & Associates Pty Ltd v. The Institute of Chartered Accountants (Aust) (2002) 122 FCR 110.
Natwest Australia Bank Ltd v. Boral Gerrard Strapping Systems Pty Ltd (1992) ATPR paragraphs 41–196.
Nauru Local Government Council v. Australian Shipping Officers Assn (1978) 27 ALR 535.
News Ltd v. South Sydney District Rugby League Football Club Ltd (2003) 215 CLR 563.
Newton v. Federal Commissioner of Taxation (1958) 98 CLR 1.
Norcat S AR L v. Bradken Ltd (No. 2) [2013] 219 FCR 14; [2013] FCA 235.
NT Power Generation v. Power and Water Authority (2004) 219 90 CLR 90.
O'Keeffe Nominees Pty Ltd v. BP Australia Ltd (1990) ATPR 41-057.
Orion Pet Products Pty Ltd v. Royal Society for the Prevention of Cruelty to Animals (Vic) (2002) ATPR (Digest) paragraphs 46-233.
Pont Data Australia v. ASX Operations Pty Ltd (1990) 21 FCR 385.
Queensland Wire Industries Pty Ltd v. Broken Hill Proprietary Co Ltd (1989) 167 CLR 177, 192.
R v. Judges of Federal Court of Australia; Ex parte Western Australian National Football League (Inc) (1979) 143 CLR 190.
Radio 2UE Sydney Pty Ltd v. Stereo FM Pty Ltd (1982) 44 ALR 557; 2 TPR 315.
Ralan St Leonards Pty Ltd v. Construction, Forestry, Mining and Energy Union [2014] FCA 431.
Re 7-Eleven (1994) ATPR paragraphs 42,644 (41,357).
Re Application by Medicines Australia Inc[2007] ACompT 4.
Re British Basic Slag [1963] 2 All ER 807, 1 WLR 727.
Re Coca Cola [1978] ATPR Com) 35-400.
Re Ku-ring-gai Co-op Building Society (No. 12) Ltd (1978) 22 ALR 621.

Re QIW (1995) ATPR paragraphs 41-438.
Re Queensland Co-operative Milling Association Ltd v. Defiance Holdings (1976) 25 FLR 169; 8 ALR 481.
Re Rural Traders Co-Op (Western Australia) Ltd (1979) 37 FLR 244.
Re Tooth & Co Ltd and Tooheys Ltd (1979) 39 FLR 1, 38-39.
Ritter v. Godfrey (1920) 2 KB 47.
Rural Press v. Australian Competition and Consumer Commission (2003) 216 CLR 53; 203 ALR 217.
Setka and Another v Magistrates Court of Victoria and Another (2017) 323 FLR 108
Shahid v. Australasian College of Dermatologists [2007 FCA 693.
Speedo Knitting Mills [1981] ATPR (Com) 50-016.
SST Consulting Services Pty Limited v. Rieson (2006) 225 CLR 516.
Strickland v. Rocla Concrete Pipes (1971) 124 CLR 468.
The Heating Centre Pty Ltd v. Trade Practices Commission (1986) 9 FCR 153.
Tillmanns Butcheries Pty Ltd v. Australasian Meat Industry Employees' Union (1979) 27 ALR 367.
TPC v. CSBP & Farmers Ltd (1980) 53 FLR 135.
TPC v. CSR Ltd [1991] ATPR 41-076.
Trade Practices Commission v. Ansett Transport Industries (Operations) Pty Ltd (1978) 32 FLR 305, 325.
Trade Practices Commission v. Australian Iron & Steel Pty Ltd (1990) 22 FCR 305.
Trade Practices Commission v. Australia Meat Holdings Pty Ltd (1988) 83 ALR 299.
Trade Practices Commission v. Email (1980) 43 FLR 383.
Trade Practices Commission v. Gillette Company (No. 1) (1993) 45 FCR 366.
Trade Practices Commission v. Nicholas Enterprises Pty Ltd (No. 1) (1978) 26 ALR 126.
Top Performance Motors Pty Ltd v. Ira Berk (Qld) Pty Ltd (1975) 24 FLR 286.
Trade Practices Commission v. Email Ltd (1980) 31 ALR 53.
Trade Practices Commission v. Parkfield Operations Pty Ltd (1985) 7 FCR 534.
Trade Practices Commission v. TNT Management Pty Ltd (1985) 6 FCR 1.
Universal Music Australia Pty Ltd v. Australian Competition and Consumer Commission (2003) 131 FCR 529.
Victoria Egg Marketing Board v. Parkwood Eggs (1978) 33 FLR 294.
Visy Paper Pty Ltd v. Australian Competition and Consumer Commission (2003) 201 ALR 414.
Wardley Australia Ltd v. State of Western Australia (1992) 175 CLR 514.
Wattyl (Aust) Pty Ltd, Courtaulds (Aust) Pty Ltd (1996) ATPR (Com) paragraphs 50-231.

Index

The numbers here refer to paragraph numbers.

Index

www.ingramcontent.com/pod-product-compliance
Ingram Content Group UK Ltd.
Pitfield, Milton Keynes, MK11 3LW, UK
UKHW020147290926
15471UKWH00004B/742